All Scripture references taken from the KJV of the Holy Bible, unless otherwise indicated.

THE WEIGHT of a MANTLE

by Dr. Marlene Miles

Freshwater Press 2026

Freshwaterpress9@gmail.com

ISBN: 978-1-971933-54-2

Paperback Version

Table of Contents

THE WEIGHT of a MANTLE

PART I: A MANTLE

WHAT IS A MANTLE

If I wanted to know what a mantle is the first thing I'd do is look it up in some type of dictionary, then go to the Bible and see what they say. Best of both worlds, a Bible dictionary. Then I'd follow the path of what was written there. This book will be about a lot more than what is in a Bible dictionary. But let's gloss over what they'd have just as a starter.

1. Hebrew *addereth*, a large over-garment. This word is used of Elijah's mantle which was probably a sheepskin (1 Kings 19:13, 19; 2 Kings 2:8, 13, etc.),.

2. Hebrew *me'il*, frequently applied to the "robe of the ephod" which was a splendid under tunic wholly of blue, reaching to below the knees (Exodus 28:4, 31; Leviticus 8:7). It was worn by priests and by kings (1 Samuel 24:4), prophets (15:27), and also rich men (Job 1:20; 2:12). So, it seems that anyone could wear whatever they wanted, or whatever they could afford.

3. *Semikah*, "a rug," the garment which Jael threw as a covering over Sisera (Judges 4:18).

4. *Maataphoth*, plural, only in Isaiah 3:22, denoting a large exterior tunic worn by females.

(1 Kings 19:13,19; 2 Kings 2:8,13,14) It seems to have been the sole garment of the prophet Elijah. It was probably of sheepskin, such as is worn by the modern dervishes.

Mantle. MAN'TLE, noun. A kind of cloak or loose garment to be worn over other garments. A cover.

Most people teach mantles like something you "catch," as if you can become that person by wearing his clothes. People think it is something someone "drops," something transferable like a jacket, but that's shallow. It's not any of those things. Mantles are covering, they do function, but they need structure.

We will discuss primarily two mantle foundations of this book.

The earth's mantle — structure. The mantle is hidden but massive. It supports everything above it. It carries movement, pressure, heat, and formation. Without it, the crust collapses. Translation: a mantle in the spirit is not decoration. It is load-bearing capacity. Earth, O Earth—we will talk about the Earth as a minister of God, discussing what it produces, what it withstands, and what it governs.

The prophetic mantle of a man. Our Scriptural anchor is 2 Kings, the story of Elijah and Elisha. That prophet's mantle wasn't magic. It represented authority, assignment, continuity of function. Elisha didn't receive a cloth; he received the capacity to carry what Elijah carried.

If the tunic or coat garment that Hannah made for Samuel was at that time called a mantle. In 1 Samuel 2:19, it says Hannah made Samuel a "little coat." That word is typically translated from the Hebrew *me'il*. That same word is also used for what we call a mantle in other places, like Elijah.

The difference is in the function.

A mantle has weight.

More than a unit of measure as it relates to gravity, *weight* is defined as the sustained demand a mantle places on a life. Weight is not pressure alone. It is not difficulty. It is not intensity for a moment.

Weight is what must be carried continuously. It is not about feelings, and it is what remains even if everything else shifts.

Weight is what your life must hold without collapse, and it never stops. It never goes away. We will find later in this book that weight is what tests and **proves** a mantle. Many think having a mantle is glorious, but trust this: there is a weight to glory even though we think of it as intangible. If we want to think of a mantle in terms of a vestment, then think this way: The train of His garment filled the temple. The Lord's garment fills space, carries presence, and cannot be reduced.

STARTING EARLY

Samuel's coat was made by his mother. It represented care, growth, and service. It was tied to his development in the house of the Lord. A mantle is not what you wear; it is what you can sustain. You don't receive a mantle—you grow into one. A mantle is proven by what doesn't break you. If it can be simply dropped on you, it can be taken from you. Most people want the mantle, but reject the weight. A mantle is not given in a moment, as in some magical or spiritual transaction; it is revealed over time. Samuel wore a coat made by his mother. Elijah carried a mantle that represented prophetic weight. The fabric, the weave or the color doesn't determine a mantle. A mantle is not material; it is intangible, and known by what it carries.

Samuel's garment equals formation environment. Elijah's mantle equals governing weight. Elijah's mantle was tied to prophetic authority. It represented weight, assignment, and function and carried as responsibility.

The same word, *mantle* can be used for a garment of care, and a garment of authority. What makes it a mantle is what it carries and what it governs. One supports development, the other requires capacity.

A mantle is defined by weight. Although intangible, a mantle has weight, but more importantly it supports *weight.*

Samuel had to study and prepare and *become* for many years to be able to carry what Eli carried. Samuel did would have to grow and be taught to be able to carry what Eli carried. He was placed in the environment, positioned under authority, exposed to function. But he still had to be formed. Even though he was called early, dedicated before birth, and in the house of the Lord, he was not yet built to carry *weight.*

Samuel's coat equals placement. Eli's role equals weight, responsibility, mantle. In 1 Samuel 3, when God first calls Samuel, he does not recognize God's voice. He runs to Eli multiple times. Samuel was present, he had access, but the boy was not yet formed and using discernment. Samuel had to grow, learn, endure time, develop discernment, and be shaped under pressure and responsibility before he could carry what Eli carried and eventually beyond it.

Placement is a start, but capacity must increase. Proximity may start, leading to readiness. Calling must be trained to grow into carrying. Being in the room does not equal carrying the weight. Being assigned early does not equal being ready immediately. A mantle is not transferred to where you are placed, it rests on what you have *become.*

Samuel had the outfit, which was called a tunic or a coat. That was called a mantle, but that was not a prophet's mantle. A mantle is not a garment, a fabric, or a prayer shawl. Lots of grown people have outfits too, but spiritual mantles are tested by weight. In God all things are tested, some even by fire.

Samuel did not inherit Eli's mantle by being near him, wearing a similar garment, or serving in the same space. He inherited responsibility *because* he became able to carry it. Samuel was in the environment before he had the capacity. He wore the garment before he carried the weight. He heard the voice before he understood it. None of that made him ready. Readiness is determined by what has been built in a person.

Pre-dedication does not eliminate the need for formation. Samuel was dedicated before birth by Hannah, placed in the house of the Lord early, and positioned under Eli. Dedication establishes direction; Hannah kept her promise and Samuel was trained up in the way he should go. Dedication establishes where a life is going, but it does not build what that life must become. His momma couldn't do that for him; Samuel had to **build** and that, under God.

He was placed early, but he was not ready early.. What is spoken over a life may be established early. What that life can carry is built over time. Others who were called did not begin by ruling. They began by being *formed*. Joseph was given dreams early, but did not step into authority immediately. He was processed through betrayal, servitude, and imprisonment before he was placed in rulership.

Daniel was taken into Babylon. There he was trained, tested, and proven before he was entrusted with influence. Jesus Christ did not begin ministry from the manger, even though He is the Son of God. Though He was the Son, and though He was sent, though He was already who He was, He spent years and years in study, and even teaching and then was baptized before He officially began. Part of the reason for that is because in that culture a man couldn't rise to ministry or certain levels until he was of age--, age 30.

There is an order to function. Calling is established early; function is not.

Joseph had revelation, way before he had authority. Daniel had position, before influence. Jesus had identity, but had not yet entered public function. None of them skipped formation. None of them bypassed process. None of them stepped into weight before they were built to carry it.

Just because something is given early does not mean that it is meant to be carried immediately. Mantles are not rushed; what a mantle requires must be built first.

There is a pattern that has already been established. Formation comes before function. Structure comes before weight. Capacity is built before responsibility is sustained. This pattern has been made obvious, yet many still try to skip it, because the process is uncomfortable.

Formation is slow, hidden, and quiet. It does not announce itself. For example, a person may attend seminary. That is a choice, but it is not a place or process where mantles are kept or gained. Formation comes into a life; it may or may not be in the process of attending and graduating seminary. There is no location that produces a mantle. There is no program that guarantees formation.

You do not enter a place to be *formed.* You are formed in what your life is required to carry. Formation is not scheduled, it is not enrolled in. There's no degree or certificate; it is lived. There is no monastery or mountain where you can go to get this *formation*.

A person can go to seminary and remain unchanged. A person can never go to a seminary or Bible college and still be *formed.* A person can go places where others consider sacred and not be affected. I was in the Holy Land with a large tour. On the plane ride back a fellow that I had met along the way was quite dismayed. He had decided that the 10-day, pastor-led, tour-led, fantastic trip to the Holy Land was a waste of his time. A person can go anywhere and never be changed. Formation is not produced by where you go. Like life, it is about your faith, expectation and in the case of mantles, capacity of what you sustain.

Formation does not respond to your plan; it responds to what your life is being built to carry. With the process of formation, there are no immediate results, no visible recognition, no confirmation that anything is happening. It is often mistaken for delay. It is not delay; it is development.

People are drawn to what is visible. Authority, influence, movement, recognition. They see the outcome, but not what produced it. They want that outcome--, specially ungoverned people.

Consistency is required when it appears that nothing is changing. Obedience when nothing is seen. Endurance when nothing is acknowledged. These do not feel like progress, so they are avoided. People look for alternatives.

Something faster. Something immediate. People look for easy. Something that feels like movement. Impartation without process. Access without structure. Position without preparation.

People compare. They see where others are and assume they can step into the same place. They do not see the years, the pressure, or what was built in private. What is visible creates desire without understanding.

Formation requires staying when leaving would be easier. Continuing when stopping would feel better. Facing what is weak instead of avoiding it. People move from place to place, moment to moment, experience to experience. Always encountering. Never building.

There is misunderstanding of what receiving a mantle really means. If something is given, it is now theirs. What is given must still be sustained. If it cannot be sustained, it will not remain.

People collect moments. Moments that felt powerful, significant, like something changed. Nothing in their life reflects the weight of what they believe they received.

The cycle continues because what is avoided must eventually be faced. Formation can be delayed, but not replaced. Weight will come. Responsibility will increase. Demand will not decrease. What has not been built will be revealed. The process cannot be skipped. It is required by reality. A mantle does not respond to desire only; it rests on what has been built. What has not been built will not carry what is real.

CARRYING MULTIPLE MANTLES?

Can a person have more than one mantle?

Yes, but with distinction. Most people think multiple mantles equals multiple powers, multiple anointings, multiple identities. This is not a comic strip; it is real life.

The truth is that a person can carry more than one mantle only if they have the structure to sustain multiple functions without fragmentation. Because each mantle is not a gift. It is a responsibility, a jurisdiction, and a weight-bearing assignment.

Moses

- Leader of a nation
- Lawgiver
- **Intercessor**

That's not three mantles randomly stacked. That is one life carrying multiple governed *functions*.

Joseph

- Dreamer and interpreter of dreams
- Administrator and very prudent steward

- Preserver of nations

Joseph's mantle *expanded* with capacity.

Elisha

- Prophet
- Governmental advisor
- Carrier of national influence

Elisha asked for a double portion of what Elijah was carrying, but that did not mean that Elisha got double titles. It was increased capacity to carry weight. You don't carry multiple mantles; you carry one life that has been stretched to handle multiple weights.

A mantle is not external. It is not transferable by force. It is not removed by circumstance. It is built, sustained, and carried internally.

A garment can be taken; a mantle cannot. People confuse clothing, symbolism, outward covering. Back in Bible times what you wore said who you were, and even today we may be like that. So, we can't confuse outfits with actual capacity and assignment. Garments are not mantles. In Matthew, a man can take your coat. He can even take your cloak. Garments are external. They can be removed. They can be given. But a mantle is not worn. It is carried.

Think of it like an internal operating system: that's your mantle. An external hard drive can be attached or unplugged depending on need. That imagery is not representative of a mantle. Said another way, if you have a heating system in your house, think of that as a mantle; it's built in. If you attach an external generator, that is not a mantle as it can be detached pretty easily, later on.

What can be taken from you was never your mantle.

THREE TYPES OF "MULTIPLE MANTLES"

1.Layered Mantles (Same Flow, Different Expressions)

Like: Teaching + Writing Prophetic + Discernment Same river. Different outlets.

2. Seasonal Mantles

A person may carry one assignment strongly in one season, then shift into another. The mantle didn't multiply—the assignment shifted.

3. Compound Mantles (Rare).

This is where it gets serious. A person carries: multiple jurisdictions, at the same time. Only because: their structure has been tested. their capacity has been proven. This is where weight becomes dangerous if misunderstood.

Most people cannot handle more than one because of the weight. Each mantle requires emotional stability, spiritual discipline and clarity of assignment. Additionally, it requires resistance to confusion, and the ability to endure pressure. Most people: collapse under one… but may seriously be asking for three.

It is not the number of mantles that matters. It is whether your **structure** can survive what you are asking God to place on you. No structure means that anything placed on you leaks out and is lost. With a weak structure, the weight of a mantle will crush. However, a strong structure can carry weight.

People believe they want mantles and more mantles for the glory. But glory has weight.

> For our light affliction, which is but for a moment, worketh for us a far more exceeding and eternal weight of glory; (2 Corinthians 4:17)

So, multiple mantles are not about **receiving more;** **t**hey are about **becoming** stronger. The Lord will not put on you more than you can bear. Yes, a person can carry more than one mantle. But only a person who has been ***built*** can carry.

PART II: THE WEIGHT OF A MANTLE

THE WEIGHT OF A MANTLE

What You Think It Is

There is a word that has been overused, misused, dramatized, and reduced to spectacle: *mantle*. People speak about it as if it is something that can be handed over in a moment, caught in a meeting, felt in an atmosphere, or received because someone stood close enough to someone else. A mantle is neither a *moment*, nor is it an accessory. It is not something you wear—neither clothing, jewelry, a big ring or a big cross necklace. It is something you carry, but you can only carry it with *capacity*.

Some have been taught to chase mantles, to go from place to place looking for the next encounter, the next impartation, or the next person who seems to be giving something they can receive. What if the problem is not that mantles are rare? What if the problem is that capacity is rare? A mantle is not proven by how it is received. It is proven by what it requires.

There are people who say they have received mantles, yet nothing in their lives can sustain weight. There is no structure, no endurance, and no stability under pressure. They speak of mantles as if they are titles. A mantle is not a title; it is a load-bearing, load-carrying reality.

If you study the Earth, you will find something hidden beneath your feet. The crust of the Earth is what is seen. It is the surface that people walk on. It carries buildings, cities, movement, and life. The crust is not what holds the Earth together. Beneath it is something deeper, stronger, hotter, and under pressure. It is the Earth's mantle.

The mantle is not visible, but it is responsible for what remains standing. It carries weight, absorbs pressure, and moves what cannot be seen from the surface. Without it, everything above it collapses.

Like the Earth's mantle in a very real sense, spiritual mantles are also not visible by the natural eye. People are looking for something visible, something noticeable, something that can be identified quickly, but the true mantle in a person's life is often the part no one sees. It is the structure that has been formed under pressure, been built over time. Solid, structurally strong but still with the ability to stand when everything around them shifts.

So, when you speak of a mantle, that is not something that sits on a person. It is something invisible that carries weight, and sustains pressure.

The Scriptures do not present mantles as performance, they present them as responsibility. When Elijah cast his mantle upon Elisha, it was not an exchange of fabric; it was the introduction of weight. It wasn't just by luck—happening to be in the right place at the right time. Elijah's mantle that rested on Elisha, wouldn't have been possible except that Elisha was prepared.

WHY MOST PEOPLE DON'T HAVE ONE

Most people do not lack desire; they lack capacity. Mantles are rare because they require something most are not willing to sustain. What is often pursued as something to receive is, in reality, something that must be built.

Many speak of mantles as if they are given in moments—through encounters, proximity, or impartation. Even if it is given in a moment it must still be sustained over time. A mantle is proven by what it requires.

Most people are not built to carry weight consistently. They may experience moments, but they cannot maintain function. They may speak with confidence, but nothing in their lives demonstrates stability under pressure. There is no structure that holds, no endurance that remains, and no consistency that continues when conditions change.

This is not a matter of calling, it is a matter of capacity. A mantle rests on structure. It functions through capacity. It produces stability. It endures over time. It governs through order.

For many are called, but few are chosen (Matthew 22:14 A)

None of these things are sustained without *formation.* Sadly, formation is what most avoid. Formation requires pressure. It requires time. It requires alignment when it is inconvenient and consistency when nothing is recognized. It requires a life to be ordered in a way that consistently supports what is being carried, continually.

This is where many withdraw.

Even though they desire what a mantle represents, they do not endure or remain for what it requires. They pursue what is visible, but they resist what is necessary to sustain it. Over time, what they claim is not reflected in what remains. A mantle cannot exist where there is no structure to support it.

This is also why many confuse *moments* with mantles. They may have a spiritual moment, experiencing something real, but they then must build what is required to carry it forward. The inspired *moment* passes, does anything remain of it? No, the experience wasn't false, but it wont last if nothing was formed to sustain it.

A mantle is not a *moment* that stays; it stays because a life has been built to sustain it. This is why Scripture emphasizes faithfulness. What a person does with little shows what they can sustain with more. Faithfulness is not about scale. It is about steadfastness.

Consistency is what most are unwilling or unable to maintain.

So, the issue is not that mantles are unavailable. The issue is that what they require is often avoided.

A mantle cannot be carried by desire alone. It cannot be maintained by language, although we will find in a later chapter that some do try to verbally insist on their mantle, but this cannot be sustained by recognition. It requires structure. It requires discipline. It requires a life that has been formed to hold weight without collapsing.

This is why most people do not have one--, not even one. Not because they were denied—but because they did not build the capacity to have a mantle.

Many want mantles. Few understand weight. And fewer still are willing to be built into something that can carry it. This book is not about how to receive a mantle. It is about what a mantle actually is. It is about why most people do not have one, even though they say they do. And it is about the difference between something that is claimed and something that can be sustained.

A mantle is not what you say you have. It is what does not collapse when pressure is applied.

Before going any further, something must be understood: you do not receive a mantle and then *become* strong. You **become** strong, and then it becomes evident what you have been carrying all along…the weight of a mantle.

THE LANGUAGE OF MANTLES

There are words that carry weight, and then there are words that once carried weight but have been used so loosely that they no longer mean anything. Mantle is one of those words.

It is spoken often, declared quickly, received easily, and repeated without definition. For all the times it is used, very few can explain what it actually is. Ask ten people what a mantle is, and you will receive ten different answers. Some will say it is an anointing. Others will say it is a calling. Some will describe it as a spiritual covering. Others will reduce it to something that can be transferred in a moment. While each of these may touch a part of the truth, none of them fully define it.

A mantle is not understood by language alone. It is understood by **weight**. The problem is not that the word exists. The problem is that the word has been separated from its substance and true meaning.

In many spaces, a mantle is treated as something that can be announced, activated, received instantly, or claimed without evidence. It is spoken over people as a declaration and accepted by people as a possession. But a mantle is not confirmed by what is said. It is confirmed by what is sustained.

Language, when used without understanding, creates illusion. And illusion, when repeated enough times, becomes accepted as truth.

So now, people speak of mantles in ways that sound right but do not hold up under pressure. They say they have received something, but there is nothing in their life that reflects the weight of it—no endurance, no structure, and no evidence of capacity. Only verbiage.

This is how confusion spreads—not because people are trying to deceive, but because words have been used without definition and repeated without examination.

There is a difference between knowing a word and understanding what that word requires.

In Scripture, the language surrounding mantles is not excessive. It is not repeated casually or explained in long definitions, yet, when it appears, it carries significance.

When Elijah cast his mantle upon Elisha, there was no explanation given. No one stopped to define the moment. No one broke it down into steps, still, everything about that moment carried meaning. Scripture often presents truth without overexplaining it. It shows you something and expects you to recognize the weight of it.

When that same moment is brought into modern conversation, it is often simplified, reduced, and turned into a formula that can be replicated without understanding what made it real in the first place.

So instead of asking, "What is a mantle?" people ask, "How do I get one?" And that question, by itself, reveals the misunderstanding. A mantle is not something you pursue as an object. It is something that becomes evident in a life that has been built.

People seem more interested in acquisition than formation and preparation to receive a mantle. They are interested in fast and easy so they focus more on experience, than forming structure. Well, as long as mantles are discussed this way, they will remain misunderstood.

If speeding up the process means that a mantle can be received without going through the proper steps, then know this: it can be lost without resistance. If it can be claimed without evidence, then it can exist without reality. If it can be spoken without weight, then it will produce nothing of substance.

This is why language must be corrected—not to control what people say, but to restore what the word, *mantle* actually means. When language is restored, expectation is corrected. Once expectation is corrected, people stop reaching for things they are not built to carry.

In the next chapter, we will address one of the most common ideas attached to mantles—that they can be transferred in a moment, given by proximity, or received without process. We will examine why that belief persists and why it continues to fail those who hold it.

We are not impressed by how quickly a mantle appears. Let us be impressed when it is proven by how well it holds.

THE MYTH OF IMPARTATION

There is an idea that has quietly shaped how many people understand mantles. It is rarely questioned, often assumed, and widely practiced. That idea is this: what someone else carries can be given to you in a moment.

This belief is built on the language of impartation, the laying on of hands, the transfer of something unseen, and the assumption that proximity creates inheritance. Because there are moments in Scripture that involve transfer, many have concluded that everything can be transferred. But there is a difference between what can be imparted and what must be built.

This is where confusion begins.

Yes, there are things that can be given; impartations can be made. Encouragement can be given. Instructions can be given. Activation can occur. Even in Scripture, there are moments where something is stirred, released, or awakened. However, a mantle is not sustained by what is given; it is sustained by what is carried. Carrying requires **structure**.

The problem is not that impartation exists, because it does. People now attend services to have encounters or *moments* expecting to receive what others have spent years carrying. They stand in rooms waiting for something to fall without asking whether anything in them can hold it. In a more macabre sense, people have been known to go to graveyards and sleep on the graves of known people who were highly anointed when they were alive, trying to receive an impartation or transfer.

This is ungoverned hunger--, doing anything for what is desired, no matter how absurd. This is misunderstanding. It is serious misunderstanding, and it is spiritually dangerous. Graveyards are dangerous, even in the daytime.

If something is truly weighty, it cannot rest on something that has not been prepared. You can place weight on a surface, but if that surface has not been built to sustain it, the result is not transfer; it is collapse.

This is why many claim to have received something, yet nothing in their life changes. There is no increase in stability, no evidence of capacity, and no ability to sustain pressure—only the memory of a moment, which can be powerful, but moments do not replace formation.

When Elijah cast his mantle upon Elisha, it was not the *beginning* of Elisha's formation, Elisha had been forming all along. Elisha did not receive the fullness of that mantle in that moment; he had previously walked away from what he knew to follow Elijah. He had followed. He had served. He had stayed with Elijah for years.

When the mantle returned to Elisha, it did not come as something new. It came as something he had already been shaped to carry.

The process of Elisha receiving this mantle is what is often removed from the conversation—the process, the time, and the proximity that produces transformation, not imitation.

Proximity, by itself, does not produce capacity. You can stand near something powerful and remain unchanged. You can observe strength and still be weak. You can witness authority and still lack structure. You can watch an exercise program… but watching it does nothing for you.

So, the idea that simply being in the room, receiving a moment, or standing under a declaration automatically produces a mantle is not supported by what a mantle requires. The idea of being in the right place at the right time as if you're catching the bridal bouquet at the wedding reception is not how this works either. That is folklore. Catching a bunch of flowers is not receiving a mantle.

Impartation can awaken. It can confirm. It can accelerate awareness. But it cannot replace the building of a life that can sustain weight.

This is why many pursue impartation but avoid *process*. Impartation feels immediate. Process feels slow. Impartation feels powerful. Process feels hidden. Impartation is seen. Process is not. You do not have to be in the presence of anyone but God to receive a mantle.

A mantle is not transferred by proximity. It is not received only by standing near someone, sitting under someone, although structure is often built by service and diligence. What is formed in a life is not given through contact. It is built under God.

God is not limited to a room, a person, or an atmosphere. What He forms does not depend on who is present. It depends on God's purposes and what has been built.

A mantle is formed in alignment, in process, in obedience, over time. It is established where a life is being shaped, not where a *moment* is being experienced.

You do not need proximity to a person to receive what must be formed within you. You need alignment with God. What is built under God will hold.

Weight requires something that is not imparted; it requires structure, which is formed, not given. This is where expectation must change. Instead of asking, "Who can give this to me?" the question must become, "What must I become to carry this?"

Other than God, no one can give you the structure of your life. No one can transfer endurance. No one can hand you stability under pressure. These things are built. And without them, whatever is received will not remain.

This does not diminish the value of impartation. It restores its place. Impartation is not the mantle. At most, it is an introduction to what may be required. This is why there are so many claims and so little evidence. What is declared in a moment must be sustained in a life. If it cannot be sustained, then it was never truly carried.

Not everything that appears powerful is built to last. A mantle is not measured by how it appears, but by what remains when the moment is over.

WHAT YOU SAW VS. WHAT IT WAS

There are moments that look powerful. They are intense. They are visible. They leave an impression. And because they are seen, they are often believed.

Could this be where many become confused. In that moment, they are not responding to what something is—they are responding to how it appeared. A moment can look like transfer. It can look like authority. It can feel like something significant has taken place. A visible moment can suggest weight without actually revealing structure. People often interpret intensity as depth, emotion as substance, and movement as power. These are not the same things. Something can be intense and still be shallow. Something can move and still not be stable. Something can feel powerful and still not be sustained.

Observation alone is not enough. What is real is not proven in a moment. It is proven over time.

When Elijah cast his mantle upon Elisha, anyone watching could have assumed that was the transfer. That was the moment everything changed. That was when Elisha received what Elijah had In our cinema-filled world, that's what most of us would have thought, but that would have been a conclusion based on sight, not on understanding.

What followed that moment was not immediate demonstration. It was process. Elisha followed. He served. He stayed in proximity—not to imitate, but to be shaped. So, the visible moment was not the full story. Whether Elisha could carry that mantle and if he had a double portion would only be proven later. A mantle is not revealed in a single moment. It is revealed in consistency. It is revealed in what remains after the moment ends, after the environment changes, and after the pressure increases. What is real does not disappear when the atmosphere shifts.

Dear Reader, comparison becomes dangerous. People compare their hidden process to someone else's visible moment. In doing so, they begin to chase what they saw without understanding what it required.

They try to reproduce the appearance without possessing the structure. The appearance of a thing can be mimicked; structure cannot. Someone can learn the language, they can mirror the tone, they can recreate the environment, but they cannot reproduce what has been built in secret. This is why imitation fails over time. What is not built cannot withstand the pressure which will be the test of everything.

What was emotional will fade. What was borrowed will collapse. What was imitated will fracture. But know this: what is built remains.

This is the difference between what you saw and what it was. What you saw was a moment. What it was, well that was the result of a life. If you only pursue what you saw, you will miss what it takes to become what it was.

A mantle is not validated by appearance. It is validated by endurance. It is not proven in a room. It is proven when the room is gone. It is not confirmed by reaction. It is confirmed by what it can carry.

Discernment is necessary because without it, anyone could misinterpret moments, mislabel experiences, and misidentify what is real. A person can call something a mantle because it looked like one. A mantle is not what it looks like; it is what it holds. What it holds cannot be measured in a moment.

A mantle is not what gives authority. It is what rests upon a life that can carry it.

THE MANTLE AS STRUCTURE

Before anything can be carried, something must be built. This is the part that is often ignored, because structure is not visible at first. It does not announce itself. It does not draw attention. It does not create immediate recognition, but structure determines everything.

If something has no structure, it cannot hold weight. If something has weak structure, it will bend under pressure. If something has been properly built, it will remain—even when what surrounds it shifts.

A mantle is not first or only a spiritual experience; it is a structural reality. This could be why many misunderstand what they are asking for when praying to *receive* a mantle. They are asking for weight without asking what must be built to hold it.

In the natural, nothing is placed on a surface that has not been tested. No one builds a house on something unstable and expects it to stand. No one adds weight to something weak and expects it not to collapse. Yet spiritually, people ask for mantles without considering the **structure** required to sustain the mantle. They are asking for something that will rest on their life without asking whether their life can carry it.

Beneath what is seen of the Earth, there is something that supports everything above it. The surface of the Earth is what people interact with. It is where movement happens. It is where life is visible, but the surface is not what holds the Earth together. Beneath it is the mantle—hidden, dense, and under pressure. The mantle carries weight that the surface cannot. It absorbs heat that would otherwise destroy. It moves in ways that are not visible while affecting everything above it. Without the mantle, the Earth's surface would not remain stable.

This is what structure does in a life. It is the part that is not seen, but it determines whether anything placed on that life can remain. When someone has structure, you may not notice it immediately. You may not see the process that formed it. You may not recognize the pressure they endured to get to where they are, but you will see the result.

This person will not collapse easily. They do not shift with every change in environment. They do not break under weight. Because something beneath the surface has been built.

This is what a mantle rests on—not talent, not desire, and not moments, but structure.

Mantles are unique and customized to a person's capacity. This is why two people can receive the same instruction and produce completely different outcomes. One builds, and perhaps the other does not. One develops stability, while the other remains inconsistent. When weight is introduced, one carries it, while the other collapses under it. One has built capacity to carry a mantle; the other has not.

The difference is not what was given. It is what was built. Structure must be in place before a mantle will arrive. If a mantle collapses it is revealing that there is insufficient or no structure in place. When weight is placed on a life, it exposes what is already there. If there is structure, the weight will settle. If there is not, the weight will scatter everything.

Collapse is the inability to sustain what they thought they had received.

Structure is formed over time. It is formed through consistency, obedience, pressure, and endurance. It is formed in moments that are not seen, in decisions that are not celebrated, and in seasons that are not recognized.

This is why a mantle cannot be understood apart from structure. Without structure, a mantle has nowhere to rest. If it has nowhere to rest, it will not remain. For those who want to carry a mantle, know this: before anything is added to your life, something must be built within it.

A mantle is not placed on *potential*. It is sustained by what has already been formed. In the next chapter, we will look at another dimension of a mantle—not just what it carries, but what it covers. A mantle both supports weight and creates environment. What it covers is just as important as what it carries.

THE MANTLE AS COVERING

The understanding on mantle deepens, because many think of mantles only in terms of what a person *does* or what they can do because of the mantle. Let's look at the presence of a mantle, or the presence of a person who carries a mantle. That they have a mantle is revealed in what surrounds them. It is indicated by what changes when they are present. It will be noticed in what stabilizes when they arrive, and what is protected when they cover.

This is the dimension of covering. A covering is not control, it is not dominance, and it is not ownership. A covering is what absorbs what would otherwise strike what is beneath it. It shields. It regulates. It creates space where something can exist safely.

In the natural, a bird does not only use its wings for flight, it uses them to cover. When a bird spreads its wings over its young, something happens immediately. The environment changes. What was exposed becomes sheltered. What was vulnerable becomes protected. What could not withstand the elements is now sustained beneath the covering.

The covering does not remove the existence of what is outside but it does absorb its impact.

This is what a mantle does. A person carrying a true mantle does not only function, but they also affect the environment around them. Things settle in their presence. Things stabilize. Things that would normally be exposed are now shielded—not because everything has changed externally, but because something has been established internally. This is why a mantle cannot be reduced to personal ability, because what it covers extends beyond the person carrying it.

In Scripture, this language is not unfamiliar. There is a consistent picture of covering as protection, shelter, and preservation. Being covered is not about being hidden from reality; it is about being protected within it.

He shall cover thee with his feathers, and under his wings shalt thou trust: his truth shall be thy shield and buckler. (Psalm 91:4)

A covering does not remove responsibility. It allows something to develop without being destroyed. Many think that covering means restriction, limitation, or control. But true covering is not oppressive; it is protective. It does not suffocate; it sustains. This is also why false coverings are dangerous. Anything that claims to cover but does not protect is not a covering. It is a weight without purpose.

A true mantle creates space. It allows growth. It absorbs impact. It regulates what would otherwise overwhelm.

This is why certain environments feel different. You can enter a space and sense stability—not because everything is perfect, but because something is covering it. You can also enter a space where there is exposure—no protection, no regulation, and you may sense everything is vulnerable in that environment. The difference is not always visible, but it is always present.

A mantle changes what is beneath it. It does not eliminate pressure, but it prevents destruction.

This is also why covering requires strength. What covers must be able to absorb what it shields. If the covering is weak, it will collapse under what it is trying to protect against. If the covering collapses, everything beneath it is exposed.

This is why not everyone can cover. Covering is not just a position; it is a function, and that function requires capacity. You cannot cover what you cannot withstand.

This is also why people must be careful what they come under. Not everything that appears to cover has the strength to protect. When pressure comes, the weakness of the covering is revealed.

A true mantle does not announce its covering. It is revealed by what remains intact beneath it—by what is preserved and by what is able to grow. Covering is not proven by words; it is proven by protection. A mantle that cannot cover is not complete. It may function. It may appear effective, but if it does not create environment, it does not carry its full expression.

A mantle does not only carry weight; it carries responsibility for what is beneath it.

THE EARTH AS A MINISTER

Before anything else is built, this must be established: the Earth is not passive. Creation does not exist without function. It operates under assignment. The Earth itself is responsive, participatory, and accountable. It does not simply sit beneath us. It functions with us.

Scripture makes this clear. In Genesis 4:10, the ground did not merely receive Abel's blood—it held testimony. "The voice of thy brother's blood crieth unto me from the ground." The Earth bears witness.

In Numbers 16:31–33, the Earth responded to rebellion. It opened, swallowed, and then closed. This is not passive terrain. This is responsive function.

In Deuteronomy 11:17, the Earth is shown to yield or withhold. It can produce or refuse. It responds to alignment. It is governed. In Matthew 18:18, what is bound or *loosed* on Earth reflects agreement with Heaven. Earth is not separate from Heaven; it is a participating realm.

The Earth does not just exist beneath us; it functions with us. Beneath the surface of the Earth is something unseen—the mantle. It is nearly 1,800 miles thick. It is load-bearing. It absorbs pressure. It sustains the crust. Everything visible depends on what cannot be seen.

This is not accidental. It is a pattern. The Earth itself carries a mantle—unseen, weight-bearing, and essential for stability. You cannot see it, yet everything you stand on depends on it. The Earth also functions as a helper. It supports life, produces food, and stabilizes systems. It serves, sustains, and responds—like a minister carrying out its assignment without announcement.

O earth, earth, earth, hear the word of the Lord. (Jeremiah 22:29)

The Earth also remembers. Blood cries from the ground. Land holds defilement. Land requires cleansing. The Earth records, holds, and testifies.

It functions as a witness. It receives actions, responds accordingly, and aligns with Truth or judgment.

A mantle, though intangible is not abstract. Even the Earth with it's own scientific mantle, carries weight. Even the Earth functions under assignment. Even the Earth sustains what is placed upon it.

The Earth was built with the capacity to carry weight. Why would you think you could carry a mantle which requires you to be able to carry weight, without structure?

This is not to say the Earth is alive like a person, but the Earth is not dead. It is to say the Earth is assigned, responsive, and structured under God. God does not create and abandon. Everything He creates has purpose, function, responsibility, and is alive.

CREATION AND THE MANTLE OF FUNCTION

A mantle is not a human idea. It is not limited to people, and it is not confined to titles. A mantle is the capacity to carry out an assignment under weight. When you look carefully, you will see that this pattern exists throughout creation, because Creation itself was not made to exist passively. It was made to function.

The Earth does not simply exist. It is not idle. It does not sit beneath you without purpose. It supports, produces, responds, and participates in what is done upon it. This is not assumption; it is shown in Scripture. In Genesis 4:10, the ground received Abel's blood and testified of it. In Numbers 16:31–33, the earth opened and swallowed those in rebellion. It responded—not randomly and not emotionally—but in alignment with what had taken place. In Deuteronomy 11:17, the earth can yield or withhold. It is not indifferent. It is responsive.

Beneath the surface of the Earth is something that cannot be seen—a vast layer that holds everything above it: the mantle. It is hidden, under pressure, and responsible for stability. Without it, what is visible would not remain. Everything above it depends on what cannot be seen.

This is not accidental. The Earth itself has been built with the capacity to carry weight. It holds, sustains, and absorbs pressure. It functions according to its assignment.

The Earth does not only carry. It remembers. What is placed upon it does not disappear. It is recorded, held, and testified. It also helps. It produces food, supports life, and stabilizes what stands upon it. It serves without announcement. It does not declare its function; it performs it.

This is the pattern. Creation carries out its assignment without confusion. The Earth does not try to become something else. It does not resist its function or reject its responsibility. It carries what it was built to carry.

This is where the parallel becomes clear. If the Earth—which is not conscious in the way you are—has been built to carry weight and function under assignment, then what do you think is required of you?

For unto whomsoever much is given, of him shall be much required. (Luke 12:48)

This is not a warning. It is a principle. What is given introduces responsibility, and responsibility introduces weight.

A mantle is not recognition; it is an assignment; it is requirement. It is the expectation that what has been placed on you will be carried—not occasionally and not when convenient, but consistently.

Creation does not negotiate its assignment. The Earth does not decide when it will function. It does not withdraw when pressure increases. It remains, and because of that, everything that depends on it is sustained.

This is the standard. A mantle is not proven by what you *say* you carry, it is proven by what you consistently sustain.

Even the Earth was built to carry weight without negotiation. What you have been given requires the same. The Earth carries weight. It does not choose when to function, and it does not withdraw under pressure. It does not negotiate its assignment. It was built to sustain what has been placed upon it, and because it was built, it can carry.

This is the difference—not assignment, but structure. Anything that has not been *built* cannot sustain what has been assigned. What you are seeing in Creation is not an exception. It is a pattern.

Understanding must shift here. You do not become capable because something is placed on you. Something is placed on you because you are capable of carrying it.

Capability is not declared; it is developed. It is formed. It is built under conditions that require stability. This is why pressure exists. Pressure is not interruption. It is formation. What is not tested cannot be trusted with weight. The Earth did not become stable when something was placed upon it. It was formed beneath the surface long before anything stood on it.

The Earth's mantle was formed under pressure, heat, and time, so is the structure within a life.

The weight of a mantle is why formation is not optional. If you are to carry weight, you must also be built. If you are to sustain responsibility, you must be formed. Without formation, assignment becomes strain, responsibility becomes burden without support, and what is placed on you will expose what is not built.

This is where we move next—into process. Because what you carry will only be sustained by what has been formed within you.

THE MANTLE AS CAPACITY

A mantle is not defined by what you desire. It is defined by what you can carry. Desire is loud. It speaks quickly, reaches far, and imagines without limitation. Capacity is quiet. It is measured. It is proven. It does not announce itself. **Capacity** determines everything.

You can desire something deeply and still not have the ability to sustain it. You can recognize something as valuable and still not be built to carry it. A mantle does not respond to desire. It rests on capacity.

Capacity is not what you say you can handle. It is what remains intact when pressure is applied. It is not measured in moments of excitement. It is measured in moments of strain.

When things are easy, many appear capable. When things are stable, many appear strong. True capacity is revealed when the weight increases, when the pressure intensifies, and when the environment shifts. This is why a mantle cannot be separated from testing. Without testing, capacity is assumed, and what is assumed is often inaccurate. In the natural, no one entrusts weight to something untested. A bridge is tested before it carries vehicles. A structure is examined before it holds load—not because there is doubt, but because weight reveals what cannot be seen.

Capacity is not formed in comfort or in ease. It is formed where something is required of you that you did not previously have the strength to sustain—and you remain. Not perfectly, but consistently.

You do not collapse. You do not withdraw. You do not abandon what has been placed before you. You adjust. You endure. You are stretched. Over time, things change. You get stronger, more able; you develop more capacity. What once felt heavy becomes manageable. What once felt overwhelming becomes structured. This is capacity. It is built through exposure to weight.

Avoiding pressure prevents growth. Without pressure, there is no expansion. Without expansion, there is no increase in capacity. Without capacity, there is no place for a mantle to rest. They say, *No pain no gain.* I know a woman who hates going to the gym because she doesn't want to sweat. So, she will use the machines and exercise up until the point of sweating, then she stops immediately. This will not build endurance or muscle tone. *No pain, no gain.*

This is also why many remain in cycles. They desire increase but avoid what would require them to grow. They want more but resist the process that would make more sustainable. So, they remain at the level of what they can currently carry—not because more is unavailable, but because more would be too much for them; it would collapse them.

This is not limitation. It is protection.

A mantle placed on insufficient capacity does not elevate a person. It exposes them. It reveals instability, inconsistency, and what has not been built. This is often mistaken for attack, but not everything that feels like pressure is opposition. Sometimes it is exposure.

If the structure is weak, what depends on it becomes vulnerable. If the capacity is insufficient, what is placed beneath it is exposed. If what is being presented as a mantle is not real, then what is to be covered is not actually protected.

This is why this is not simply a personal matter. It is not only about whether a person can carry weight. It is about what happens to those who rely on that weight being carried.

A false mantle does not only collapse a person. It destabilizes what was built around it.

A borrowed mantle cannot sustain others, because it is not sustained within the person carrying it.

An unsustained mantle does not fail quietly. It reveals itself over time through what it can no longer hold.

This is why capacity matters. Not for position. Not for recognition, but for responsibility.

Because what you carry does not only affect you. It affects what is placed under you. When what is carried cannot hold, everything connected to it feels the strain.

This is not limitation; it is protection.

Not everything withheld is denial. Some things are not placed because what would depend on them would not survive.

This is why capacity must be developed intentionally—not for recognition, and not for expansion alone, but for sustainability. A mantle is not proven by how much you can access. It is proven by how much you can sustain without collapsing, fragmenting, or becoming unstable.

Capacity also determines reach—what you can carry personally and what you can carry for others. You do not want to be responsible for collateral spiritual damage. A mantle does not only carry weight; it also covers. And you cannot cover what exceeds your capacity. You cannot sustain others if you cannot sustain yourself.

This is why growth must be internal before it becomes external. Before influence expands, capacity must increase. Before responsibility multiplies, structure must deepen. Expansion without capacity is not increase. It is overload, which will sooner or later, break.

This is why some rise quickly and fall just as fast—not because what they received was false, but because what they had built was not sufficient to sustain it.

A mantle will never exceed the capacity of the one carrying it without consequence. Either capacity rises to meet the weight, or the weight reveals the lack of it.

This is why the focus must shift from, "How do I receive more?" to, "How do I become able to carry more?"

Because increase is not something that happens to you. It is something your life must be able to hold.

Once capacity is present, what you carry will no longer feel foreign. It will feel fitting, because you have been *built.*

In the next chapter, we will move into formation more directly—not just what a mantle is, but how a life is shaped into something that can carry one. Capacity does not simply appear. It is not inherited; it is developed. What is developed can sustain what is real.

PART III — HOW A MANTLE IS FORMED

BUILT UNDER PRESSURE

Woe to them that are at ease in Zion...(Amos 6:1)

No mantle is formed in ease. It is not developed in comfort, and it is not established in convenience. It is not produced in environments where nothing is required. A mantle is formed under pressure.

This is the part most people avoid—not because they do not want the mantle, but because they do not want what produces it. Pressure is not pleasant. It does not feel like progress or promotion. It feels like demand. It may feel like oppression or attack. It requires more than you are used to giving. It stretches what you thought was enough and exposes where you are not as strong as you believed.

Because of this, many misinterpret pressure. They see it as opposition, assume it is unnecessary, and try to escape it as quickly as possible. But pressure is not always an enemy. Sometimes it is the very thing forming you.

Without pressure, nothing is strengthened. Without resistance, nothing is built. Anything that has been formed to carry weight has been shaped under conditions that required it to hold. In the natural, materials are tested under pressure before they are trusted with responsibility—not because they are expected to fail, but because what cannot endure pressure cannot be trusted with weight.

This is also true in a life. You are not entrusted with more because you desire it. You are entrusted with more because you have demonstrated that you can remain when something is required of you. Pressure reveals this. It reveals how you respond when things are not easy, whether you remain when things become difficult, and whether your structure holds when something presses against it. This is where formation takes place—not in what you say you can do, but in what you continue to do when it becomes costly.

Pressure introduces cost. It requires time, endurance, and decisions that are not always comfortable. In those moments, something is being built—not always visibly and not always immediately, but consistently.

This is why many abandon the process too early. They feel pressure and assume something is wrong. They feel stretched and assume they have missed something. They feel the demand increasing and interpret it as a sign to withdraw, but often, it is the opposite.

The pressure is not there to destroy you. It is there to form you into something that can carry more than you could before. This does not mean all pressure is correct, but it does mean that pressure itself is not the problem.

The question is not, "Is there pressure?" The question is, "What is this pressure producing?" If it is producing instability, collapse, and confusion, something is wrong. But if it is producing endurance, strength, clarity, and stability under strain, then something is being built that is increasing capacity.

This is why pressure cannot be separated from mantles. Without pressure, there is no proof of what can be carried. Anyone can say they are ready. Anyone can believe they can handle more, but pressure reveals the truth. It shows what holds, what bends, and what breaks. What breaks must be rebuilt stronger if it is to carry weight.

This is also why pressure often comes before recognition; you are being proved. Recognition without formation creates exposure. If something is seen before it is *built*, it will be placed under weight prematurely, and that weight will reveal what has not yet been formed.

So, formation must come first—quietly and consistently, under conditions that require growth. This is where many are shaped without being seen, without being announced, and without being recognized. But what is formed there does not disappear. It becomes the very thing that allows a mantle to rest.

In the next chapter, we will go further into this process. Because pressure alone is not the only element. There is also heat. There is time. There are hidden places where formation continues without visibility. And what is formed there will determine what can be carried in the open.

HEAT, TIME, AND HIDDEN PLACES

Pressure begins the process, but it is not the only thing that forms capacity. There is also heat. There is time. There are hidden places where formation continues without visibility. This is where most people lose interest. Because nothing in this stage is seen. Nothing is announced. Nothing appears to be happening. Yet, this is where some of the most important work is done.

In the natural, the Earth's mantle is not only under pressure, it is also under heat. The heat is constant. It is not occasional. It is not seasonal. It is sustained. This combination of pressure and heat, over time, creates movement, density, and strength beneath the surface.

The Earth's upper mantle is hot. It is at least 1000 degrees Fahrenheit. The lower mantle is even hotter at up to 7000 degrees Fahrenheit. The mantle is also under extreme and intense pressure. We could never experience those temperatures, but sometimes under the pressures of life, things can feel intense for us.

We don't have to do what the Earth itself does, but the layer that carries everything we stand on was formed under heat most could not endure. Without heat, the mantle would not function as it does. Without time, the process would not be complete. This is how formation works in a life. It is not a single moment and not a single experience. It is sustained exposure to conditions that shape you over time.

Heat represents intensity that does not immediately pass—situations that linger, circumstances that do not resolve quickly, and things that require you to remain even when you would prefer to move on. This is where endurance is built—not in what comes and goes, but in what stays.

Time allows formation to settle. What is formed quickly is often not stable. What is rushed is rarely deep. But what is formed over time becomes part of the structure. It is no longer external. It becomes internal. This is why time cannot be bypassed. It is not delay; it is development.

Hidden places are where this process occurs—not in front of people and not in environments where everything is visible, but in places where no one is watching, nothing is being acknowledged, and there is no external validation.

This is where many struggle. Without visibility, it feels like nothing is happening. Without recognition, it feels like no progress is being made. Formation does not require visibility. Some of the strongest structure is built where it cannot be seen. How many of God's leaders received formation in a cave or on the backside of a desert?

What is built in hidden places is not dependent on external response. It is not shaped by reaction and not influenced by attention. It is formed in consistency.

Motives are revealed here. When nothing is being seen, why do you continue? When nothing is being acknowledged, why do you remain? When there is no immediate outcome, what sustains your commitment?

These are not distractions. They are part of the formation.

A mantle cannot rest on something that depends on visibility to function. It cannot rest on something that requires constant recognition to remain steady. It must rest on something that has been built to stand regardless of who is watching.

Hidden places produce stability, consistency, and independence from external affirmation. This is also where refinement happens. Things are removed. Things are adjusted. Things are strengthened—not through public correction, but through internal alignment.

This is why hidden seasons are necessary—not as punishment and not as delay, but as protection. What is being built must be able to stand when it becomes visible. If it is exposed too early, it will be tested before it is ready, and what is not ready will not withstand what comes against it.

So, it is formed in hidden places first—under heat, under pressure, and over time. It's not a quick process, but it is a necessary one. A mantle is not sustained by moments. It is sustained by what has been formed in places no one saw. What has been formed there will not disappear when everything becomes visible.

In the next chapter, we move further into this process. Formation is not only about what is added. It is also about what is removed, which is just as important as what remains.

THE SEPARATION PROCESS

Formation is not only about what is added. It is also about what is removed. This is where many become unsettled, because addition feels like progress and increase feels like movement, while removal often feels like loss.

Things begin to shift. Connections change. Access is reduced. What was once familiar no longer fits. Without understanding, this can be misinterpreted. It can feel like something is being taken, like something is being withheld, or like something has gone wrong.

But in many cases, nothing has gone wrong. Something is being separated.

Not everything can remain if weight is to be introduced. A mantle requires space—not physical space, but structural space. If a life is already filled with conflicting priorities, unstable patterns, and unnecessary attachments, there is nowhere for weight to settle.

So, separation becomes necessary—not to isolate you from purpose, but to remove what interferes with it.

This is not always dramatic. Sometimes it is subtle—a gradual distancing, a quiet shifting, or a loss of interest in what once held your attention. Doors close. Opportunities change. Relationships no longer align.

This is where many try to hold on. They attempt to maintain what is familiar and preserve what is comfortable. But if what is being removed cannot remain without affecting what is being built, then it must be removed.

Everything in your life contributes to your structure. If something weak remains connected, it will affect your ability to carry weight.

This is why separation is not rejection. It is refinement. It is the process of removing what cannot remain if something greater is to be sustained.

Then said he, Lo, I come to do thy will, O God. He taketh away the first, that he may establish the second. (Hebrews 10:9)

In the natural, before something is built to carry weight, it is cleared. Unstable material is removed. Obstructions are taken out. Anything that interferes with stability is addressed. It doesn't matter if what is removed has value or not, if it cannot remain in that structure, then it must go. This is what separation does. It removes what does not belong in what is being built.

This is also why separation can feel personal, because it touches areas that have been part of your life. This is not about attachment. It is about alignment. What remains must align with what you are being built to carry. What does not align cannot remain without consequence.

This is where discernment is required. Not everything that leaves is meant to be restored, and not everything that feels like loss is actually loss. Sometimes it is release. Sometimes it is adjustment. Sometimes it is the removal of what would have weakened what is being formed.

Timing also matters. Something may have been appropriate in one season but cannot remain in another—not because it has changed, but because you have. What you are becoming requires a different structure.

This is where resistance must be addressed. If you resist separation, you delay formation. If you hold on to what is being removed, you create instability, which will not support weight. This does not mean everything must be cut off abruptly, but it does mean everything must be evaluated.

Does this align with what is being built? Does this strengthen my structure, or weaken it? These are not casual questions. They determine what remains. A mantle cannot rest on a life that is divided. It cannot be sustained where there is constant conflict between what is being built and what is being held onto.

Separation creates clarity. It simplifies structure. It removes interference. It allows what is being formed to settle properly. While it may feel like reduction, it is actually preparation. What remains after separation is what can support what is coming.

In the next chapter, we will move into a different kind of challenge—not what is being formed, but what is falsely claimed. Once formation begins, it becomes easier to recognize what is real and what only appears to be real.

PART IV — FALSE MANTLES

COUNTERFEITS

The enemy of our souls has counterfeits or nearly everything God has made. In the devil's attempt to mimic mantles, in the natural, we see images of wizards, magicians, vampires, and the like often wear capes in stories, in the movies and sometimes in real life.

Remember, a real mantle is an assignment that requires capacity and responsibility and affects the environment by bringing covering. It is earned through formation. It is proven by what can be sustained.

It is not an outfit; and an outfit won't cut it.

Counterfeits don't build—they signal. What you're seeing in stories (wizards, magicians, vampires with capes) is not a true "mantle." It's a symbolic shortcut.

Capes and cloaks show up. In storytelling, a cloak or cape communicates instantly: authority, power, status, separation from ordinary people. It's visual language. Writers use it because it *signals* something without explaining it.

The difference is that a real mantle is invisible, it is structural. It is proven over time. It requires discipline

Fictional “mantles” (capes and cloaks are visible. They are immediate, symbolic and require no formation.

Counterfeits emphasize appearance, while real mantles depend on capacity.

This pattern exists because human beings instinctively understand covering as authority. They see garments as a role or position. Clothing is function and also identity in some cases. This is why uniforms matter. We recognize doctor’s coats, judges’ robes, military dress and graduation gowns, for example.

Stories borrow that instinct and exaggerate it.

What’s the “counterfeit” in real life? Not capes necessarily. But things like titles without substance are signals and not real. Declarations without discipline are not real. Association mistaken for authority is fake. Performance replacing consistency cannot be depended upon. These *look like* authority… but don’t carry weight.

As a Biblical parallel, keeping it simple, in Matthew 23: People loved the outward appearance… but lacked substance.

For there is no respect of persons with God. (Romans 2:11)

This is why we are not a respecter of persons. A real mantle does not need to be seen. It must be sustained.

Stories use visuals because real mantles are invisible, internal, and proven over time. Stories need something immediate. Costumes represent what can’t be shown quickly. They go to Wardrobe Central to find an outfit to reflect humanity’s instinct to represent authority visually although that authority is not from God, but from some other source. All authority not from God is counterfeit.

A real mantle is not worn as an external garment--, not as a garment at all. It is carried within. It is not ego.

FALSE COVERINGS

Images Without Structure

Not everything that looks like a mantle is a mantle. Better said, not everyone who looks like they are carrying a mantle is. This is where confusion increases, because there are coverings that appear to represent authority but do not carry it. They signal something, suggest something, and resemble something, but they do not sustain anything.

Across cultures and throughout history, coverings have been used to represent role, authority, and function. Robes, garments, and uniforms are not random. A judge wears a robe. A soldier wears a uniform. A graduate wears a gown. These communicate position, assignment, and responsibility. The garment does not create the role. It reflects it. *Clothes do not make the man, the man makes the clothes.*

The problem begins when the image is treated as the substance—when appearance is mistaken for capacity, and what is visible is assumed to be what is real. This is where false coverings emerge. They present the form of authority without the structure required to sustain it.

A false covering can be seen immediately, recognized quickly, and assumed easily, but it cannot hold weight because nothing has been built beneath it. When weight is applied, what is real will remain, and what is not will begin to collapse—not gradually or subtly, but inevitably. Appearance cannot support responsibility.

Association can create false coverings, and this is not always intentional. A person may be near something real, connected to something established, and familiar with its language and expression. Over time, they may begin to assume that proximity equals possession. They start to function as if something has been placed on them when nothing has been built within them.

Announcement can reinforce this. Words can affirm what has not been formed. Something can be declared and accepted before it has been established. Once accepted, it can be carried outwardly as if it were real.

A false covering can exist in environments without pressure. It can be maintained where nothing is required. But when responsibility increases, when consistency is required, and when something must be sustained, the difference becomes clear.

What is not built cannot hold. A real mantle does not depend on visibility. It does not require recognition to function. It is proven by what remains consistent under demand. **A false covering, however, requires environment, reinforcement, and recognition. Without these, it cannot be maintained.**

This is why images are not enough. Symbols can communicate something, but they cannot carry it. A garment can represent authority, but it cannot produce it.

The distinction is clear. A real mantle is carried within. A false covering is displayed without.

What you wear can suggest authority. What you sustain reveals it. What is not built cannot carry, and what cannot carry cannot remain. This is not about recognition. It is about responsibility. Once something is truly placed on a life, responsibility is no longer optional; it must be sustained. It's like, whatever you did to get your spouse, you must keep doing to *keep* your spouse. This is where many fail—not at the level of appearance, but at the level of requirement.

A real mantle does not ask, "Can you be seen?" It asks, "Can you **remain**?"

What is placed on you introduces expectation—not from people, but from the weight itself. Weight demands consistency. It does not adjust to your preference. It does not reduce itself because you are tired, and it does not disappear because it is inconvenient.

It remains, and so must you.

This is responsibility—not title, not language, and not association, but the ability to sustain what has been entrusted to you without collapse.

A mantle does not become real because it is named. It becomes evident because it is carried consistently.

Why would someone loudly insist they are a prophet and say to others that they "wouldn't know one if they saw one"?

That behavior is usually not about authority. It's about validation and control of perception. REAL AUTHORITY does not need volume. It does not need defense. It does not demand recognition. It is demonstrated through function, over time. This person is overly assertive because they need to be declared. By verbalization, by their words they intend to create the perception they want people to believe. Then to keep up that perception, they need to defend and react to every perceived challenge. Why? Because they are not really established; they are false.

What's happening internally, often (not always), one or more of these are present:

- Insecurity about legitimacy.
- Dependence on external recognition.
- Confusion between calling and formation.
- Frustration that results are not matching claims.

So, the response becomes: "Say it louder so it feels more real. What has to be insisted upon repeatedly is often not yet established. This does not mean every bold person is false, or that every quiet person is real. It means that volume is not evidence.

A person who must announce, defend, insist. They may be trying to establish through words what has not yet been proven through function. Perhaps what they want to prove may not even be provable. It could be blatantly false. A mantle does not need to be defended. It will be revealed by what it sustains.

Titles that require defense are usually false titles. Not every title reflects a mantle. Some titles must be maintained through insistence. Repeated. Reinforced. Defended. Titles that require defense must be protected externally. A title that requires defense is one that has not yet been proven through function. So it must be: stated often, emphasized strongly, and protected quickly. Without reinforcement this false title or false assignment begins to weaken.

They have a need to be recognized. Recognition becomes necessary when structure is not yet present. So, the focus shifts from what is being carried, to what is being acknowledged. This is where insistence appears. Insistence is only required when something is fake, false, not true, or uncertain. Sometimes that is seen in has-beens who want to make a comeback, or linger past their season. Sometimes it is simply seen in charlatans.

Reaction reveals instability. When their assumed title is challenged, the response becomes defensive, immediate and emotional. The challenge is not really being evaluated; it is being resisted.

What is real does not require defense. A real mantle is not maintained by agreement. It does not depend on recognition. It is revealed by what it sustains over time. Consistency becomes the witness. Not volume. Not repetition. Not insistence.

The difference is that a title can be **given,** but a mantle must be **carried**. A title can be announced, whereas a mantle must be sustained. A title can be defended. A mantle will be demonstrated.

What must be protected by words has not yet been secured by structure. There is a difference between being called and being built.

MANTLE ENVY

Wanting What You Are Not Built to Carry

Not every desire is alignment. Some desires are comparison. Some are observation without understanding. Some are the result of seeing what another carries without seeing what it requires. When you don't know what a person went through to get to where they are in life, that should give you pause and keep you from coveting. Even if they went through it, doesn't mean you can; it doesn't mean that everyman or any man can. They were called to that and God gave them Grace to persevere. When you are not called to something, don't do it. Don't try it.

Mantle envy is not admiration. It is the desire to carry what has not been built within you. It looks at another life and concludes, "I should have that," without asking, "What does that require?"

What is visible is often attractive—authority, influence, and function. What is *not* visible is what made it possible: formation, pressure, consistency, and endurance. Mantle envy sees the outcome. It does not see the structure.

This is where misalignment begins. When a person attempts to carry what they have not been built for, called for, Graced for, or anointed for, one of three things happens: they strain, they imitate, or they collapse. Weight does not adjust to desire. The weight that is coming to test that mantle – it is not something that the uncalled person can endure.

Consider Mephibosheth and Samson. They were not built for the same function. Mephibosheth was sustained under covering, while Samson was built for confrontation. To desire one while being built for the other is to step outside of alignment.

Envy distorts perception. It makes another assignment look preferable, another capacity look attainable, and another life look easier. But in reality, you are not seeing the full weight.

This is why envy is dangerous—not because of emotion, but because it leads to misplacement. A person begins to pursue the wrong function, abandon their actual assignment, and measure themselves incorrectly. Over time, what they were built to carry is neglected.

You cannot borrow capacity. Capacity is not transferable. It is developed. What another has built cannot be adopted through desire.

The correction is simple. The question is not, "What do they have?" It is, "What have I been built to carry?" Because alignment does not come from comparison. It comes from clarity.

The Earth is mostly mantle; the surface (crust) is extremely thin. The mantle is ~1,800 miles thick while the curst is on 5 to 30 miles thick. What actually supports everything we see on the surface is mantle (and core). The part we live on is the smallest part of what holds us. Surface

= visible. Mantle = hidden and load-bearing. Most of what matters cannot even be seen. Less than one percent of the Earth is visible surface. Everything else is what makes it stable. The Earth is overwhelmingly mantle. The surface is a thin layer resting on something much deeper

A spiritual mantle does not exist to elevate you, it exists to fulfill an assignment that shifts, completes, or reach its limit or the end of its season.

You must not compete with others.

You must not compete with what comes next.

He must increase, but I must decrease.

He that cometh from above is above all: he that is of the earth is earthly, and speaketh of the earth: he that cometh from heaven is above all. (John 3:30-31)

Decrease is not diminishment. It is the refusal to compete with what has been established. You do not become less. You remain aligned when your assignment is no longer central.

- John prepared
- Christ established

So "decrease" means do not overextend your mantle. It doesn't mean to hold position beyond assignment. Do not compete with what has been fulfilled. Do not try to keep alive that which is already fulfilled and whose season has ended. Do not attempt a comeback on something that is over.

But stay aligned in the Lord.

Moving on after a season is not false humility. Nor is it hiding, silence, or weakness. This is clarity. It is restraint and alignment; it is completion

Decrease is not about becoming smaller. It is about not remaining where your assignment has ended. Yes—but not as self-erasure. It is alignment with what has already been established in Christ

A mantle does not give a person flashy ability, and it is not instant power. It is not exceptional moments, although Scripture says that those who know their God will be strong and do exploits. A mantle, however, gives capacity for consistent function, ability to sustain responsibility and stability even while under pressure and weight, over time

This is not a SUPERPOWER because it is not bursts, drama, spectacle, and moments of display. What matters is what can be sustained. A mantle doesn't give a superpower, it gives the capacity to function consistently under weight. A mantle is not about what you can do once. It is about what you can sustain repeatedly.

Samson had moments of extreme strength, but lacked consistent structure. The result was collapse.

Daniel was not spectacle. There were no bursts, but decades of consistency. That is a mantle. Power can appear in moments. A mantle is proven over time. Power is what can happen. Mantle is what can be sustained. Again, a mantle does not give a *superpower*, it gives the ability to carry, function, and remain—consistently.

Not a superpower, not a title, but a pattern of consistent function that is specific to their assignment is what will happen. A mantle produces a recognizable pattern. What is unique is not occasional ability. It is not isolated moments. It is what repeatedly happens through that person, and around them, over time. What is unique is not what they can do once, it is what consistently happens *through* them.

Daniel's pattern:

- interpretation,
- stability, and
- governance under pressure

Joseph's pattern:

- administration
- preservation
- provision in crisis

John the Baptist's pattern:

- preparation,
- alignment, and
- redirection toward Christ.

None of these are "superpowers." They are; however, consistent functions tied to assignment. What makes it unique, is not that others *can't ever* do it… but that this person sustains it at a level thar others do not. A mantle does not make something impossible for others. It makes it consistent for the one who carries it.

This is why people notice it. They don't always say that's a mantle. They say this always happens with them. They may say something like, "They are always able to accomplish this, that, or the other, **in Christ**." They may notice that things always stabilize when they are present or speak to the condition or situation.

That's the pattern speaking.

A Talent = occasional.

Gift = situational

Mantle = consistent, sustained pattern.

What is unique is not ability, it is consistency of function under weight. What is unique **to the person** is the consistent, sustained pattern of function tied to their assignment.

These are the things that people may see and begin to covet another's gifts, skills, talents, abilities, anointing, or even the mantle they carry.

However, when envy is removed, A person becomes stable, focused, and consistent. They stop reaching outward…to people but upward to God, and then they begin building inward. Envy reaches for what is visible. Alignment builds what is required. You cannot carry another man's mantle. And you cannot sustain what you were not built to hold.

WHAT A MANTLE GOVERNS

A mantle does not exist in isolation. It governs by what comes into alignment under its presence. It does not require weighty titles or strong declarations.. GOVERNANCE IS THE EVIDENCE. Authority is not proven by what is said.

Not by might, nor by power, but by my spirit, saith the Lord of hosts. (Zechariah 4:6B)

It is proven by what is maintained. If nothing is brought into order… nothing is being governed.

A real mantle does not create confusion. It produces order, consistency, and stability. Things begin to function properly. Not because they are forced… but because they are aligned. This is not control. Governance is not domination, it is not manipulation. It is not pressure.

It is alignment. What is out of order comes into order. What is unstable becomes steady. What is inconsistent becomes reliable. A mantle may govern: a life, a household, a people, a system, but regardless of scale… the evidence is the same.

Order is established.

When nothing is governed nothing is being stabilized… if nothing is being sustained… if nothing is coming into alignment… Then nothing is being governed which means there is no functioning mantle.

Consistency is the sign. What is governed does not fluctuate constantly. It does not collapse under pressure. It remains. Because it is being maintained.

This is why time reveals truth. In the short term… many things can appear ordered. Over time… what is not governed will begin to break down. Governance must be continuous, not momentary.

A mantle is not proven by activity. It is proven by what it keeps in order. Where there is no order, there is no governance; where there is no governance, there is no mantle.

The man with fine clothing shows up to an event. A well-dressed man is honored, while a poorly dressed man is treated as lesser.

> If there come unto your assembly a man with a gold ring, in goodly apparel… and there come in also a poor man in vile raiment; and ye have respect to him that weareth the gay clothing… (James 1-4)

What's happening here is that value assigned by appearance. Authority assumed by presentation. Too many times, preference given without substance, or proof of substance. This is what can happen with false coverings. A person can get fine clothes almost anywhere, even if he steals them. A fancy person can find fancy vestments and march in wearing them. That doesn't make them real.

That person, or any other, for that matter can take the HIGHEST SEAT at the event, or in the house. this is self-exaltation. Really, why would he be wearing the fancy clothes, except for self exaltation?

Well, that man can take the high seat, but later, he may be asked to step down.

When thou art bidden… sit not down in the highest room;
lest a more honourable man than thou be bidden…
and thou begin with shame to take the lowest room.

For whosoever exalteth himself shall be abased;
and he that humbleth himself shall be exalted. (see Luke 14:7-11)

James 2 talks about misplaced recognition. People honor what *looks* like authority Luke 14 — Self-Assigned Position. People can assume (or try to assume) a position they have not been built to hold. Recognition can be misplaced. In James, a man is honored because of what he wears— not because of what he carries.

In Luke, a man takes a higher seat— only to be removed from it. What is assumed by appearance will eventually be corrected by reality.

A seat can be taken, but only **structure** determines whether it can be held.

BORROWED MANTLES

Not everything that looks like a mantle is one. Some things are carried for a time… but were never built into the person carrying them. This is what can be called a borrowed mantle.

It appears real. It functions for a moment. It may even produce a response. But it is not sustained. Because it was never formed within the life carrying it. A borrowed mantle is not always intentional. It does not always come from deception. Sometimes it comes from proximity. Being near something long enough to learn how it looks. How it sounds. How it moves. And over time, what is observed is repeated.

Language is learned. Patterns are copied. Expressions are mirrored. And eventually, it can appear as if something has been carried.

Appearance is not structure. And imitation is not formation. This is where many become convinced they have something real… because they can reproduce what they have seen.

They can speak the same way. They can respond in similar patterns. They can create environments that resemble what they observed. Resemblance is not evidence. When what has been borrowed has not been built, it will not be sustained.

Borrowed mantles fail under pressure. When pressure is applied what was learned externally is not enough to hold what is required internally. Pressure does not respond to appearance. It responds to structure.

So, this is where things begin to break down. Consistency fades. Stability weakens. What once seemed strong begins to fragment. Not because something was taken… but because nothing was established.

A borrowed mantle relies on environment. It functions best in familiar settings. Where the same conditions exist. Where the same responses are expected. Remove the environment and the function disappears. If it was never internal is will not hold. If is was only supported externally, or propped up, it will fail. This is why some appear effective in one place… and ineffective in another. When what they are carrying is dependent on where they are when they change locations, that's it. A true mantle is not environment-dependent. It remains consistent regardless of where it is placed. Because it is built into the person.

This is also why borrowed mantles often seek validation or make bold declarations. They require response. They depend on recognition. They need confirmation to continue, because without external reinforcement, there is nothing internal sustaining them. This is not strength; it is dependence. And dependence cannot carry weight. This is also why borrowed mantles are often exposed over time. Not immediately and not always in obvious ways. But gradually. Because time removes what is not built. It reveals inconsistencies.

It exposes instability. It shows where something cannot be maintained. What cannot be maintained cannot be called a mantle. This is where humility becomes necessary.

It is possible to operate in something borrowed without realizing it. I think of people who brazenly copy another person's business (let's say they used to work there). They are copying it because they now that that it is done this way and only this way. They have no understanding of the deep workings of business. In the same way a church may split and another may start, they are not led or directed by God, they are simply copying something they saw before. Both of these are borrowed mantles. When pressure or weight comes. Well ---.

To function in patterns that were learned but never developed. When that is recognized, the response must not be denial. It must be correction. Because what is borrowed can be released to create space for what can be built.

This is the difference between imitation and formation. Imitation copies what is seen. Formation builds what is real. Only what is real can sustain weight. A borrowed mantle may look convincing… for a time.

Pressure and time will always reveal the difference. What is borrowed cannot remain. Still, not all false mantles are borrowed; some are declared. Some are spoken into existence without the structure to support them. What is declared without structure does not become real just because someone said it.

ANNOUNCED MANTLES

There are mantles that are formed. And there are mantles that are announced. These are not the same. An announced mantle is something declared before it is established.

It is spoken. It is affirmed. It is sometimes celebrated, but it is not yet supported by structure. This is where language becomes dangerous again. Because words can create the appearance of reality… without the presence of it.

Something can be spoken over a person: "You carry this." "This is on your life." "You have received this mantle." If that word is accepted without examination, it can become a belief.

Belief does not equal capacity. Truth is, if someone tells you that something is 'on your life' you may figure there's nothing else to do. I already have this.'

Declaration does not create structure. This can be very confusing to receive a word… and assume it is complete. A person could hear something spoken… and treat it as established. A mantle is not confirmed by declaration; it is confirmed by what can be sustained.

This does not mean that every word spoken is false.

There are moments where something is identified, recognized, and even released. But what is spoken must still be *built*. A word does not replace **formation**. It may point to something, and it may reveal direction. If a true prophet is speaking, or whomever is speaking under the anointing, they may be seeing a future event.

So, speaking it does not remove the *process* required to carry what has been spoken. This is where imbalance occurs. Some people receive a word… and begin to function as if the structure already exists. They move ahead of formation. They step into weight they have not yet been built to carry. What happens next is predictable. Instability. Inconsistency. Collapse under pressure. Not because the word was wrong… but because the structure was not ready.

This is why timing matters. Something can be true… and still not be established. Something can be spoken accurately… and still require development. This is where maturity is revealed. A mature person does not rush to perform what has been spoken. They submit to the process that makes it sustainable. They do not try to prove the word. They allow their life to grow into it. This is the difference between announcement and formation. Announcement speaks ahead, prophetically. Formation builds underneath. If formation does not follow announcement… what was spoken may not come to pass, but if it does, it will not remain.

This is also why announced mantles often create the kind of pressure that forces performance. The expectation to demonstrate something that has not yet been developed to appear as if something is already present… when it is still being formed.

This is not growth; this is strain Over time, it brings fatigue, produces inconsistency, instability, and eventually, collapse. When the life is trying to support something that has not yet been built into it will end in disaster. This is also why some begin strongly… and then disappear. It may not even mean that they weren't called. The word may not have been false, but that word could have been announced prematurely before structure was formed.

This is where patience becomes necessary—not passive waiting, but active development. It is allowing structure to be built, allowing capacity to increase, and allowing endurance to be established so that what was spoken can eventually rest on something real. When formation is complete, announcement is no longer needed. What is present speaks for itself. There is no need to declare it or prove it, because it is evident in what is sustained.

An announced mantle depends on words. A formed mantle does not.

In the next chapter, we will continue examining false mantles, because not everything that appears real comes from declaration. Some things come from association—from being near something and assuming that nearness equals possession.

ASSOCIATION AND PROXIMITY

There is another way mantles are misunderstood—not through imitation alone and not through declaration alone, but through association. It is the belief that being **near** something means you carry it. This is subtle, and because it is subtle, it is rarely questioned. People assume that if they are close to it, around it, or connected to it, then they must also have it. Proximity is not possession.

You can be near something powerful and remain unchanged. You can sit in environments where weight is present and still not have the structure to carry it. You can be connected to someone who carries a mantle and still not carry one yourself, because mantles are not transferred through association; they are sustained through formation.

This is where many confuse access with capacity. Access allows you to see. Capacity allows you to carry. These are not the same. You can have access to something without having the ability to sustain it.

Proximity can create false confidence. Being around something repeatedly can make it feel familiar, and what feels familiar can be mistaken for something internal. But familiarity is not formation. It is exposure which by itself, does not produce structure. Recall, Saul was in the company of the prophets and began to prophesy. Saul was not a prophet, but he was proximal to them. There is such a thing as association of spirits, but it is temporary.

This is why two people can be in the same environment and leave with completely different outcomes. One is changed, and the other is not. One builds, and the other observes. One develops capacity, and the other develops language. The difference is not proximity. It is about what is done with what is seen.

Association can also become misleading because others may assume that if someone is connected, they must carry the same thing. Connection does not equal capacity. Being *aligned* with something does not mean you have been built to carry it.

This is where identity becomes unstable. A person begins to define themselves by what they are near instead of what has been formed within them. When that proximity changes, so does their sense of identity, because it was never rooted in structure; it was rooted in association.

This is also why some lose direction when they are no longer in certain environments—not because something was taken, but because nothing had been established internally. What they relied on externally was never developed within them, and without that internal structure, there is nothing to sustain them.

This is not a failure of environment. It is a misunderstanding of what proximity produces. Proximity can expose you to something. It can allow you to observe. It can give you the opportunity to learn, but it cannot build capacity for you. That must be developed.

This is why being near something should not lead to assumption. It should lead to evaluation. What in you is actually changing? What in you is actually being built? Not what you have seen or experienced, but what has been established within you that can remain when you are no longer there.

Because if it cannot remain, it was never yours.

A true mantle is not dependent on proximity. It does not require a specific environment to function, and it does not disappear when conditions change. It is not sustained externally. It is built internally, **under God.**

This is where independence is formed—not independence from people and not isolation, but independence from the need to rely on external environments to maintain what should exist within.

A mantle must remain regardless of where you are placed. It must function without constant reinforcement. It must hold without continual support.

Otherwise, it is not a mantle; it is dependence. Proximity must be understood correctly because dependence cannot carry weight. Yes, it is an opportunity, but it is not a guarantee. Use every opportunity well because what you do with that chance determines what is formed within you.

PART V — GUARDING THE MANTLE

GUARDING WHAT YOU CARRY

Structure, Boundaries, and Sustained Weight

What you carry must be maintained—not occasionally and not when it is convenient, but consistently. A mantle does not sustain itself. It is sustained by what is maintained around it. Some assume that what they carry will protect them automatically. Others assume that they must constantly defend it. Both are incorrect.

You do not guard a mantle like an object. You guard alignment, discipline, structure, and responsibility, because these are what allow it to function.

When structure is maintained, what you carry begins to establish order, create boundaries, define what is allowed, and remove what is not sustainable. This does not happen through effort, but through function.

A mantle "protects" by operation, not by intention. When something is properly governed, what is out of order cannot remain.

You will not always need to say, *No, Stop*, or *This cannot continue,* because what you carry will not support it.

Over time, what is incompatible will either adjust or leave. This is responsibility—not control, not pressure, and not performance, but the consistent maintenance of what allows weight to be carried. When this is neglected, if alignment weakens, discipline declines, and structure is not maintained, then what you carry will begin to suffer—not because it was taken, but because it was not upheld.

You do not guard a mantle directly. You guard what allows it to function. Maintain the structure, and what you carry will establish the boundaries.

A mantle does not elevate you. It obligates you. This is where understanding must become honest. Too many are drawn to mantles for what they believe they will gain. Influence. Visibility. Authority. Contrary to popular belief, a mantle does not exist to give you something; it exists to require something from you.

Responsibility cannot be avoided. Whatever you carry comes with what you are responsible for sustaining. Consistently. A mantle does not turn on and off. It does not adjust to your preference. It does not step back when you are tired. It remains.

Responsibility is not emotional. It does not respond to how you feel. It does not adjust to whether you are motivated. It requires consistency. It exposes discipline, stability, and endurance. It doesn't respond to what you *say* you can do… but what you actually sustain over time. This is why responsibility feels heavy. It is constant and you must remain constant, as well.

It does not wait for the right moment. It requires you to show up when nothing in you feels like it. This is the weight. The presence of the mantle is not the weight; it is intangible, the weight is in the requirements of the one carrying it.

It demands alignment, order, and discipline. It requires that certain things be maintained. It demands that your structure remains intact. Furthermore, it requires that your capacity continues to increase.

If you are inconsistent… what depends on you becomes vulnerable. If you neglect what you carry… what is connected to it is impacted. This is why a mantle is never only personal. It always affects more than the one carrying it. Responsibility cannot be casual, because what is at stake is not limited to you. It includes whatever and whoever is under your *covering.*

This is where maturity becomes necessary--, day after day. This is also why some begin to withdraw after initially stepping into responsibility. The weight is constant. If they were only drawn to desire a mantle by what they thought they would gain… they will not prepared for what is required. This is when you find people pulling back. Discipline fades. Structure becomes unstable. Then, over time, what was once carried can no longer be sustained.

And Jesus said unto him, No man, having put his hand to the plough, and looking back, is fit for the kingdom of God. (Luke 8:62)

Once a mantle is carried…it will require something from you every day. If you are not prepared for that… you will eventually resist what you once pursued. **Responsibility is the weight**. If you're in it for the 'glory' – well, there is a weight to that glory, but as heavy or heavier than that is the requirement to remain aligned with what you carry. Every day.

This is what separates those who sustain mantles from those who do not. It is not access, not moments, but the willingness to remain responsible when it is no longer easy.

In the next chapter, we will go further into this weight. Because responsibility exposes something else. Weakness. When real weight is applied, weakness does not remain hidden. That is when it is revealed.

WHEN RESPONSIBILITY IS NOT MAINTAINED

A mantle is not handled the same way in every case. Some things cannot be taken, but they can be neglected, forfeited, or replaced.

Reviewing, a mantle is assignment, capacity, and responsibility. It is not an object, so it cannot be handled like something external. It cannot be stolen. No one can take your formation, your capacity, or what has been built within you. What is built cannot be transferred by force. A mantle also cannot be worn temporarily like a garment. It is not something you put on and remove at will. It is carried through structure.

What, then, can happen? This is where clarity matters.

A mantle can be neglected. When discipline weakens, alignment shifts, and responsibility is not maintained, what is carried begins to suffer—not because it was removed, but because it was not sustained.

A mantle can be forfeited through disqualification. Consider Saul. He was appointed, but through disobedience and misalignment, he lost his position. The assignment continued, but not with him.

A mantle can be replaced. What Saul could not sustain was carried by David. The role did not disappear. It moved to someone who could carry it.

A mantle can also be laid down or completed. This is not failure, but fulfillment. John the Baptist said, "He must increase, but I must decrease." His assignment reached its conclusion, and he remained aligned to it.

A mantle can be misused. Samson had real capacity but handled it poorly. The result was weakening, exposure, and eventual collapse.

A mantle is not lost like an object. It is either sustained or not, aligned or not, carried or not. It is not taken from you; it is either maintained, or it is no longer carried by you.

Neglect weakens function. Misalignment disrupts stability. Disobedience disqualifies. Completion concludes assignment. Faithfulness sustains and increases.

What is real is not lost suddenly. It is revealed over time by what is or is not sustained.

This understanding protects against extremes—the idea that nothing can ever happen to a mantle, or that everything can be taken from you. Neither is true.

Responsibility determines continuity.

Situation	What Happens
Neglect	weakens function
Misalignment	disrupts stability
Disobedience	disqualifies
Completion	concludes assignment
Faithfulness	sustains and increases

WHEN A MANTLE IS NO LONGER CARRIED

A mantle is not visible; it is intangible. It cannot be touched, and it cannot be handed over as an object. Yet its presence—or its absence—is evident.

A mantle is known by what it sustains, not by what is claimed and not by what is remembered, but by what continues to function under its weight. When a mantle is carried, order is maintained, responsibility is sustained, and consistency remains. When it is no longer carried, those things begin to change.

It does not disappear suddenly. A mantle is not removed like a garment. It is revealed over time through what is no longer sustained. What was once stable, consistent, and ordered begins to show gaps, inconsistency, and instability when it is no longer maintained or carried.

This change is not always seen immediately. At first, it may not be obvious, because memory can maintain an image long after function has weakened. Reputation can continue even when structure has declined. But over time, what is not being carried will no longer hold.

Neglect weakens function. When alignment shifts, discipline declines, and responsibility is not maintained, what was once sustained begins to suffer—not because it was taken, but because it was not upheld.

Misalignment disrupts continuity. A mantle functions within order. When alignment is lost, what was once consistent becomes unstable. The structure may remain, but the function begins to break.

Disobedience can disqualify. There are moments when responsibility is not only weakened, but removed. Consider Saul. He was appointed, but through disobedience, the authority continued without him.

This is critical. When a mantle is no longer carried by a person, the assignment does not disappear. It continues. What Saul could not sustain, David was built to carry.

Many are the plans in a man's heart, but the counsel of the Lord shall remain. (Proverbs 19:21)

Even if you don't want to do something or complete something, God's plan will remain. He has others.

Yet I have left me seven thousand in Israel, all the knees which have not bowed unto Baal, and every mouth which hath not kissed him. (1 Kings 19:18)

Not every ending is loss; many are success. Some mantles are carried until their purpose is fulfilled. John the Baptist said, "He must increase, but I must decrease." That is not collapse; that is completion.

Misuse weakens what is real. A mantle can be real and still be handled poorly. Samson carried strength but misused it. The result was not immediate loss, but gradual weakening. That was then followed by exposure.

The distinction is clear. A mantle is not lost like an object. It is no longer carried when what it sustains is no longer maintained.

You do not know this by announcement, but by observation. What is no longer consistent? What is no longer stable? What is no longer sustained? Absence is not declared. It is revealed. A mantle does not leave loudly. It is shown quietly by what no longer holds. When the weight is no longer carried, the structure will reveal it.

A mantle is not retired; it is fulfilled. Some mantles are lifelong. Some deepen over time. Others are seasonal or very specific in function. When the work is complete, the weight does not need to remain the same. So then, remain in alignment with God, enter into a season of rest when appropriate. You're not stepping away from responsibility. You're recognizing when a specific responsibility has been carried to completion.

Give God the Glory!

WHEN WEIGHT EXPOSES WEAKNESS

Weight does not create weakness. It reveals it. This is one of the most misunderstood parts of carrying anything real. When pressure increases… when responsibility expands… when something heavier is placed on your life— Whatever is already there becomes visible.

Weight is not only pressure, exposure, or correction, but it can also be confirmation, expansion, or even trust. Weight functions to show when the structure is not ready or if there is instability. It shows weaknesses, as we've discussed as well as strain.

Weight as confirmation shows things remaining steady with no collapses or fractures.

Not all weight is pressure; some weight is trust. *Lean on me, when you're not strong…* Know this: What breaks one person may establish another.

If there is strength, it will show. If there is instability, it will show. Not because the weight caused it… but because the weight exposed it. This is where many misinterpret their experience. They begin to feel the strain. They begin to see cracks. They begin to encounter difficulty, so they assume that something is wrong. When this happens, the question needs to be: “What is being revealed in me?”

Weight exposes inconsistency, lack of discipline, emotional instability, areas where structure was never built and anything else that was hidden. These things may not have been obvious before. In lighter conditions, they can remain unnoticed. They can be managed. They can be hidden. But when weight is applied… they cannot remain concealed.

This is why increase often feels uncomfortable. It confronts what has not been developed. It reveals where growth is still needed. If this is misunderstood, it leads to one of two responses: Withdrawal or denial. Withdrawal says, “This is too much. I need to step back.” Denial says, “There is nothing wrong. This is not an issue.” Truthfully, neither response produces growth. Withdrawal avoids the exposure. Denial ignores it. In both cases, what has been revealed remains unchanged.

This is why exposure must be handled correctly—not as condemnation or failure, but as information. It shows you where structure is weak, where capacity must increase, and where something must be strengthened.

This is also why weight must be applied progressively. Too much exposure at once can overwhelm, but measured exposure allows for adjustment, strengthening, and growth. This is how capacity increases—not by avoiding weakness, but by addressing it, reinforcing what has been exposed, and building where there were gaps.

Discipline and humility are both necessary at this point, because exposure requires acknowledgment. You must be willing to see clearly and say, “This is not as strong as I thought. This area needs to be built.” Without that acknowledgment, nothing changes, and without change, capacity does not increase.

This is why some remain at the same level—not because they are incapable of growth, but because they resist exposure. They avoid situations that reveal weakness. They stay within what is comfortable. As a result, what is weak is never strengthened.

So, when greater weight is introduced, they are not able to sustain it.

Weight will always find weakness. When it does, it gives you an opportunity—not to retreat and not to deny, but to build. Because what has been exposed is now visible, and what is visible can be strengthened. This is how growth happens—not in what is already strong, but in what has been revealed as weak. Over time, what was once unstable becomes steady. What once could not hold becomes reliable.

This is the purpose of exposure—not to disqualify you, but to prepare you to carry more without collapsing.

In the next chapter, we will take this further. Weakness alone, is not the only reason people collapse. There is something more foundational—the absence of structure itself. When that is missing, no amount of desire can compensate for it.

PART VI: THE BURDEN...

WHEN WEIGHT EXPOSES WEAKNESS

There comes a point where understanding is no longer theoretical, where definitions are no longer enough, and where explanations no longer satisfy. Once a mantle is understood, what remains is not curiosity. It is weight. It's not the kind of weight that can be discussed lightly or carried casually, but the kind that demands something from the one who bears it.

A mantle is not an idea. It is not a concept. It is not a spiritual language that can be spoken without consequence. It is a burden—not in the sense of something unwanted, but in the sense of something that must be carried consistently.

This is where many turn back. It is one thing to understand a mantle. It is another thing to live under its requirement. The burden does not adjust to you. It does not become lighter because you are tired, and it does not become optional because you are unwilling. It remains.

This is the dividing line between those who speak of mantles and those who *carry* them. Speaking requires nothing, but carrying requires everything.

It requires your alignment, your discipline, and your consistency. It requires that your life be ordered in a way that can sustain what has been placed on it. The burden is not just what you carry. It is what you are responsible for maintaining—what you must remain aligned with and what you must not neglect.

The weight becomes clear right here. It's not in the moment of receiving or recognition, but in the daily requirement to remain consistent with what you carry.

Many focus on the *moment* and not the maintenance. They are drawn to what appears powerful or glorious, but are unprepared for what must be sustained.

When the reality of the burden becomes clear, they begin to resist what they once desired—not openly, but gradually. Consistency weakens. Discipline fades. Alignment shifts. Over time, what was once carried can no longer be sustained.

When the burden was not maintained a life can become misaligned with it. So, the burden must be understood—not as something heavy to avoid, but as something real to respect. Because once you carry something real, it will require something real from you—not occasionally, but continually.

This is where maturity is revealed—not in what you say and not in what you receive, but in what you sustain day after day.

The burden is not proven in a moment. It is proven in consistency. In the test of consistency is where many are separated—not by lack of desire and not by lack of opportunity, but by lack of endurance.

The burden does not lift itself; it is carried.

Only those who are willing to carry it will sustain what it requires. From here, we move deeper into the burden itself. The weight does not only require responsibility, it exposes, it tests, and it reveals what is built and what is not. Once the burden is present… nothing remains hidden for long.

Weight presents to reveal weakness. When the weight increases and something in them begins to strain, they assume something has gone wrong. The presence of strain is not always a sign of failure, it is often a sign of exposure.

Weight uncovers what lighter conditions concealed. In ease, many things appear stable. In comfort, many things seem strong, but when something real is placed on your life, what is actually there begins to show. This is revelation.

What is weak does not become weak in that moment. It was already weak. It simply had not been required to hold anything substantial, so it remained hidden. But when weight is introduced, there is no place for it to hide.

It exposes inconsistencies you could previously manage, disciplines you never fully established, and areas where structure was assumed but never built. This is why increase often feels disruptive because it reveals what must be strengthened. Even if it's something good, it is still a revealer.

Now, exposure is not always attack. They feel the pressure, see what is being revealed, and conclude, *"This is too much. This is not right."* At that point, they begin to withdraw. Or they might do something just as dangerous--, they deny what has been revealed. They explain it away, minimize it, and refuse to acknowledge it. Neither of those acts will tend to stability. Withdrawal avoids the weight, denial ignores the weakness. In both cases, nothing is built or restored.

Exposure is not there to disqualify you, it is there to show you what must be strengthened if you are to carry what has been placed on your life. Know this: What is revealed can be reinforced, but what is ignored remains unstable.

Responsibility must return. Once something is exposed, you are now accountable for it—not to feel bad about it and not to be discouraged by it, but to address it. You are to build where there are gaps and strengthen what has been weak.

This requires honesty; you must be able to say clearly, *"This area is not as strong as I thought. This must be developed."* Without that level of clarity, growth won't occur. This is also why weight must be handled progressively. Too much exposure at once can overwhelm a person who is not prepared. Whereas, measured weight reveals in stages, allowing time to build, adjust, and strengthen.

Capacity will increase by addressing weakness directly. Over time, what was once unstable becomes steady. What once could not hold becomes reliable because structure increased or improved. Exposure, as inconvenient as it seems, if you are honest and address it head on, will prepare you to carry your mantle well.

A mantle is not proven by how much you can access. It is proven by how much you can sustain without collapsing. So, weight must not be feared. It must be understood. When it exposes weakness, it is also revealing the next place where you must be built.

In the next chapter, we will go deeper. Exposure alone does not explain why some collapse completely.

WHY MOST PEOPLE COLLAPSE

Collapse is not sudden but often it appears that way. What appears to be a sudden failure is often the exposure of something that was never built. Those who think collapse is an all of a sudden thing will say that the pressure was too much, the attack was too strong, or the timing was wrong.

I can compare this to a dental crown that comes out. The patient invariably says, I was just eating something soft. That is true. Something hard broken the cement seal, but it was something soft, maybe days later that attached to and lifted that crown off that tooth. Something soft seemed to be sudden, but it was not. The cement seal was broken or weak, first.

If something collapses under weight, the issue is not the weight. The issue is the absence of structure. Anything that has been built properly does not collapse when weight is applied. It may strain, it may be tested, and it may require reinforcement, but it does not fall apart.

Collapse happens when there is nothing beneath the surface that can sustain what has been placed above it.

Collapse is often misunderstood as failure. But collapse is not failure. It is exposure. It shows clearly that there was no structure there.

This is difficult to accept because it challenges assumptions. It confronts what was believed to be present. Clarity is necessary, because without it, nothing will be rebuilt correctly.

Some appear strong for a time. They function, they move, and they produce visible results. It seems as though everything is in place, but what is visible is not always supported. There may be activity without structure and movement without foundation. As long as the weight remains light, this can continue. Later, when real weight is introduced, everything changes. What was functioning externally is now required to be supported internally. If there is nothing there, collapse is inevitable.

Yet, time and pressure reveal truth. They remove the illusion that something is stronger than it really is.

Collapse can feel overwhelming because it is not just one area that fails. It is everything that depended on what was not built. When structure is absent, there is nothing to stabilize the system. When one part gives way, the rest follows.

This is logical; it is reality. Weight requires support, and where there is no support, there is nothing to hold it. This is also why recovery must begin with honesty—not explanation, not justification, but clarity. You must be able to say, of yourself and your own situation – we are not judging others--, "This was not built." Not partially built, not weakened, but absent. If you misidentify the problem, you will misapply the solution. You will try to reinforce something that does not **exist.**

Therefore, rebuilding must go deeper—not to surface adjustments or external corrections, but to the establishment of structure where there was none. This takes time, intention, and consistency, but it is the only way to ensure that what collapsed does not collapse again.

When understood correctly, collapse can become a turning point—not an ending, but a correction. Once you see clearly what was missing, you can begin to build it. So, what is built properly does not collapse under the same weight.

That is the difference between repeating cycles and establishing stability.

This is the most common scenario where people collapse is not because they were attacked and not because they were targeted, but because what they were carrying was not supported by what had been built.

Once that is understood, everything changes. The focus shifts from "How do I avoid collapse?" to "How do I build something that cannot be collapsed?"

That is where stability begins.

In the next section, we move into a different kind of understanding. Once structure is established, the question is no longer collapse, it is expansion which introduces a new challenge—not survival, but capacity for increase.

PART VII: MULTIPLE MANTLES

ONE LIFE, MANY WEIGHTS

The question is often asked: can a person carry more than one mantle? The answer is yes, so now we will go a little deeper than we did at the outset of this book.

People often imagine multiple mantles as separate identities, separate roles, or separate expressions that exist independently. A mantle is not a collection of parts. It is a function of a life. When a person carries more than one mantle, they are not carrying separate things. They are carrying multiple weights within one structure.

This is where clarity is necessary, because without it, people begin to divide themselves. They attempt to operate in fragments, separating functions that should be unified. As a result, they become unstable, because a divided structure cannot sustain compounded weight.

A person is not designed to become multiple versions of themselves. They are designed to become strong enough to carry multiple demands within one life. This is the difference—not multiplication of identity, but expansion of capacity.

This is why structure must deepen before weight increases. Each additional responsibility does not sit beside the others. It rests on the same foundation. If the foundation is weak, adding more will not expand the life; it will overload it.

This is where many make a critical error. They assume that if they can handle one, they can handle more. But handling one does not automatically mean they have the structure for multiple, because weight does not increase linearly; it compounds.

Each additional demand interacts with the others. It requires more consistency, more discipline, and more stability—not the same level, but a greater one. This is why expansion must be measured—not by opportunity, but by capacity. Opportunity will always exceed capacity if it is not evaluated. Accepting what exceeds your capacity does not produce growth; instead, it produces strain.

This is also why some begin well and then fragment—not because they were incapable, but because they expanded too quickly. They added responsibilities without reinforcing structure. When pressure increased, everything began to compete for stability. Focus divided, consistency weakened, and structure strained. What once functioned well became difficult to sustain. This is not because multiple mantles are wrong. It is because capacity was not increased before weight was added. This is also why some are given more gradually—not because more is unavailable, but because more must be supported. I don't mean to wear this out, but support requires structure.

As weight increases, discipline becomes more critical. What was optional becomes necessary. What was flexible becomes fixed. What was occasional becomes consistent. Multiple weights require greater order.

Clarity must also increase, because confusion cannot coexist with compounded responsibility. If direction is unclear, everything becomes unstable. A person carrying multiple weights must be clear in function, stable in structure, and consistent in execution—not occasionally, but continually. What they carry does not pause.

This is why not everyone should pursue multiple mantles—not because it is not possible, but because it requires more than many are willing to sustain. It requires a life that has been built to handle increased demand without losing alignment.

If alignment is lost, everything is affected.

This is the difference between expansion and overload. Expansion increases capacity along with responsibility. Overload increases responsibility without increasing capacity. Only one of these is sustainable.

A person carrying multiple mantles is not doing more. They are built differently. Their structure has been strengthened, and their capacity has been expanded. What would overwhelm another, they can sustain—not because it is lighter, but because they are stronger.

This is the key—not how much you carry, but what your life has been built to sustain.

In the next chapter, we will go further. Expansion introduces a serious risk—the desire to increase before capacity is ready. When that happens, what could have been sustained becomes something that cannot be carried.

CAPACITY BEFORE ADDITION

Why increase is dangerous without structure

Increase is not always progress. This is where many become misaligned, because opportunity feels like advancement—more responsibility, more visibility, more access. Because it is more, it is assumed to be better. However, more is only beneficial if it can be sustained, otherwise, it becomes dangerous.

This is the part that is rarely considered, because addition is appealing. Increase feels like movement, growth, or even success. It feels like something is happening, but what? Addition without capacity does not build a life; it destabilizes it.

Every addition introduces weight, and weight must rest on something. If structure is not reinforced before addition, what is added will begin to strain what already exists.

This is how instability begins. Symptoms of it do not show up immediately or always visibly, but it will be realized internally. Pressure increases, focus divides, and consistency weakens. What once functioned well begins to feel difficult to maintain.

This is not because the addition was wrong, but because the structure was not ready. Any increase must be evaluated carefully—not by desire and not by opportunity, but by capacity. Ask yourself these questions: *Can this be sustained consistently? Can this be carried without compromising what already exists?*

If the answer is unclear, then the addition is premature. This does not mean it is not meant for you at all, but perhaps not right now. *Why?* Because this means that it is not yet supported.

Restraint becomes necessary at this point. Not every open door should be entered immediately, and not every opportunity should be accepted. What you accept, you become responsible to carry, and responsibility does not adjust to your level of preparation.

Some lives become overloaded with too many responsibilities, too many demands, too many things requiring attention. Eventually, something begins to fail when a person exceeds their capacity. What was intended to be expansion is not that at all if there is nothing to rest it on. In that case, it is only accumulation.

So, capacity must come first. Structure must be reinforced. Consistency must be established. Discipline must be maintained so that when addition comes, it has somewhere to rest. When capacity is present, addition does not strain. It settles and integrates. It becomes part of the structure instead of a disruption to it.

Sustainable increase happens this way, by becoming able to carry more. Until that ability is present, addition remains a risk.

In the next chapter, we will see the other side of this. When expansion is real, it does not feel like overload. It feels like alignment. As long as there is alignment whatever is added can be carried without breaking.

A mantle is not what gives authority. It is what rests upon a life that can carry it.

WHEN EXPANSION IS REAL

How true growth actually occurs

Real expansion is not forced. It is not rushed, and it is not driven by opportunity alone. It is the result of capacity meeting responsibility. This is the difference between growth that is real and growth that is assumed. Real expansion does not strain the structure. It fits it.

When capacity has been developed, increase does not feel foreign. It feels appropriate—not easy, but fitting.

Real expansion does not disrupt what is already established. It strengthens it. What was already consistent remains consistent. What was already stable remains stable. Nothing begins to collapse because something new has been added. Instead, the structure holds. You can expect this when capacity was increased **first**. The life was built before the weight was added. So, when the weight arrives, it does not create instability. It reveals readiness.

Genuine expansion often appears gradual each increase is absorbed, and each addition is integrated. Nothing is forced beyond what can be sustained. This is what makes it lasting. What is built correctly does not need to be adjusted constantly; it holds.

Real expansion also produces clarity, not confusion. When something fits, there is no internal conflict. There is alignment. You know what must be done and what must be maintained. There is no competition between responsibilities which is another mark of true growth. That mark is order. Expansion without order creates chaos, but expansion **with** order creates stability.

Authentic expansion does not require constant validation. It does not need to be announced or proven, because it is evident in what is sustained. This is the difference between appearance and reality. Appearance requires attention. Reality does not. It remains whether it is seen or not.

How and that a mantle holds proves it is the genuine article. When expansion is real, what is added becomes part of what is carried without weakening the life that carries it. This is because the structure was already built. What is built properly can always support what is added to it.

PART VIII — DISCERNMENT

WHAT A REAL MANTLE PRODUCES

Stability, not spectacle

A mantle is not proven by how it appears. It is proven by what it produces.

Discernment must become clear here, because many evaluate mantles based on what they see in a moment—intensity, movement, and reaction. While these things can be present, they are not proof. A mantle is not measured by spectacle. It is measured by stability.

Spectacle draws attention. It is visible, immediate, and creates response. Stability remains. It is consistent, reliable, and does not depend on reaction to exist. Something can be spectacular and still be unstable. It can produce a moment but not sustain a life. What is stable, however, continues beyond the moment. It holds. It does not collapse when the environment changes, and it does not weaken when attention is removed. It remains.

Remember, stability is the first mark of a real mantle—stability under pressure. It must remain stable and have consistency that does not break when weight is applied. This is also why a real mantle is often less visible than people expect. It is not always dramatic. It does not always announce itself or draw attention, but it is evident over time—in what is sustained and in what does not collapse.

Spectacle can be misleading because it can be created. It can be produced intentionally and repeated. But stability cannot be manufactured. It can only be built. What has not been built will not remain consistent.

Time removes what is not real. It reveals what cannot be maintained and exposes what depends on environment, attention, or response. What remains after time and pressure is what is real.

A real mantle also produces order, not confusion. Things are clear, aligned, and sustained properly. Stability creates structure, and structure produces order.

real mantle does not create chaos. It does not produce instability in what it touches. It brings things into alignment—not by force, but by consistency.

This is also why what is real can be trusted. Not because it is impressive, but because it is reliable. It does not change unexpectedly or shift without reason. It remains consistent under different conditions.

This is what makes it stable.

Stability is often overlooked. It is not dramatic. It does not demand attention or create immediate reaction. But it is the very thing that allows everything else to function. Without stability, nothing can be sustained.

This is why a real mantle must be evaluated correctly—not by how it looks in a moment, but by what it produces over time. Does it remain consistent? Does it withstand pressure? Does it create order?

These are the questions that matter.

Because what produces stability is built, and what is built can carry weight. Everything else, no matter how impressive it appears, will eventually be revealed as something that cannot be sustained.

In the next chapter, we will go deeper into discernment. Production alone is not enough. We must also examine endurance—not just what something produces, but what it can withstand over time.

WHAT A MANTLE CAN WITHSTAND

Endurance as evidence

Production reveals something. Endurance confirms it. It is one thing to produce. It is another thing to remain. This is where many misjudge what is real. They see what something produces and assume that is enough. But production without endurance is incomplete.

What is real does not only function. It lasts.

Endurance is the evidence that what has been built can withstand what comes against it consistently over time. Even when pressure returns, it stands, because endurance is not proven in ease. It is proven when conditions are not favorable, when opposition is present, and when demand does not decrease. What is carried does not stop.

This is the measure—not how something performs when everything is aligned, but how it holds when things are not. Endurance cannot be imitated. It cannot be created quickly or produced on demand, because it is the result of something that has been built to remain under strain. Time is necessary in this proving. Endurance is not visible immediately. It is revealed over seasons, through consistency, and through repeated pressure. What remains after time has passed is what is real.

Some appear strong initially and then fade—not because they lacked ability, but because they lacked endurance. They could produce, but they could not sustain. A mantle is not proven by what it does once, but by what it continues to do without breaking. Endurance requires alignment. What is aligned holds and remains consistent even when pressure is applied.

Endurance is not passive; it is active consistency with a continued ability to remain intact under ongoing demand. This is what proves a mantle—not how it begins, but how it continues. What continues without collapse is what has been built.

In the next chapter, we will complete this section. A mantle does not only produce and does not only endure. It governs.

WHAT A MANTLE GOVERNS

Authority proven through order

A mantle does not only carry weight. It establishes order. This is where authority is revealed—not in what is said and not in what is claimed, but in what is governed.

Authority is not proven by declaration. It is proven by what comes into alignment. Many associate authority with position, title, and recognition, but these things do not establish order; they announce it. A mantle, however, governs. It brings things into alignment without needing to force them. It establishes consistency, creates structure, and stabilizes what was previously unstable. This is how authority is recognized—not by how loud it is and not by how visible it is, but by what changes when it is present.

Governance is the final evidence. What a mantle produces, and what it withstands, must result in something: order. If there is no order, there is no governance. If there is no governance, there is no authority. This is the measure. What does it bring into alignment? What does it stabilize? What does it maintain consistently? These are not theoretical questions. They are observable. What is governed does not remain chaotic. It becomes structured—not rigid and not controlled, but aligned.

This is also why false authority fails. It may appear strong, but it does not produce order. It may speak loudly, but things remain unstable. It may demand response, but nothing is sustained. Authority cannot exist where order is absent.

A real mantle does not need to assert itself constantly. It does not need to prove itself, because what it governs speaks for it. Things remain stable. Things function properly. Things do not collapse under pressure. This is the evidence—not what is claimed, but what is maintained.

Governance requires responsibility. What is brought into alignment must be maintained. Order is not established once. It is sustained in that consistency. This is where authority becomes ongoing—not an event, but a function. It is a continual ability to maintain alignment under changing conditions. This is what a mantle governs not people alone and not systems alone, but order itself.

Where order is maintained, authority is present. This is the final layer of discernment. What is real produces stability. What is real endures. What is real governs. And anything that does not do all three, no matter how it appears, cannot be called a mantle.

Upcoming: In the final section, everything comes together. Because understanding alone is not the end. The question that remains is simple: what will you do with what you now understand?

PART IX — FINAL WORD

YOU DON'T RECEIVE IT — YOU *BECOME* IT

What was assumed has been examined. What was misunderstood has been corrected. What remains now is not information; it is understanding. The question is no longer, "How do I receive a mantle?" Instead, it is "What must I become to carry one?"

A mantle is not something that arrives fully formed on a life. It is revealed in a life that has been formed. This is the shift—from receiving to *becoming*.

Everything points to the same conclusion. A mantle rests on structure, functions through capacity, produces stability, endures over time, and governs through order. None of these things are given in a moment. They are developed. They are built. They are formed through pressure, time, and alignment.

A mantle cannot be separated from the life carrying it. It is not external; it is integrated. It becomes part of how you live, how you respond, and how you remain.

There is no moment where everything is complete. What you carry will continue to require something from you—not to prove it, and not to perform it, but to sustain it.

This is where many must decide. Not whether they desire a mantle, but whether they are willing to live in a way that can carry one. desire is easy, but *becoming* requires everything. It requires alignment when it is inconvenient, discipline when it is not desired, and consistency when nothing is recognized. It requires that your life be ordered in a way that supports what you carry—not occasionally, but continually. This is the cost. Not something added to your life—but something that shapes your life.

Not everyone is meant to carry the same weight. And not everyone is willing to become what is required. This is not limitation; it is alignment. What you are built for is what you will be able to sustain, all else will fall away.

A mantle is not proven by what you say you have. Nor is it proved by showing off to everyone --, *Hey look at me, look what I have*. Or, *Look what I can do*. It is proven by what your life can sustain without collapsing. When that becomes true, there is no need to announce it, declare it, or prove it. It will be evident in what remains. In what holds. In what does not break under pressure.

This is the final understanding: You do not receive a mantle and then become something. You *become* something…and it becomes evident what you have been carrying all along.

YOU DON'T RECEIVE IT—YOU BECOME IT *(with Scripture anchor)*

By now in this book, the language has been cleared. What was assumed has been examined. What was misunderstood has been corrected. What remains is not information. It is understanding. And understanding changes the question.

Scripture does not present mantles as objects people collected. It presents lives that were formed to carry weight.

Consider Elijah and Elisha. Elisha did not step into Elijah's mantle because he witnessed a moment. He followed. He served. He remained. When the mantle fell on Elisha, it did not make him something new. It revealed what he had *become* capable of carrying.

Consider Moses. He did not begin as a leader of a nation. He was formed in obscurity, in separation, and in responsibility that seemed small. Over time, he became someone who could carry people, pressure, responsibility, and divine instruction. The mantle did not create Moses. Moses was built to carry what was placed on him.

Consider Joseph. He was given dreams early, but he was not ready to carry what they meant. So, he was processed through betrayal, delay, and hidden places until he became someone who could sustain authority without collapsing under it. The position did not form him. The process did.

Consider David. He was anointed early, but he did not step into the throne immediately. There was time. There was pressure. There was testing. The anointing was a declaration, but the mantle required formation. Only when he had been built could he carry what had been spoken.

This is the pattern.

In every case, the word came early. The formation came after. And the mantle became evident only when the life could sustain it.

A mantle cannot be separated from *becoming*.

It is not something external placed on a person. It is something internal that has been built over time.

This is why Scripture says in Luke 16:10, "He that is faithful in that which is least is faithful also in much..." Faithfulness in small things is not about small things. It is about structure. What you do with little reveals what you can sustain with much.

In 1 Corinthians 4:2, we read It is required in stewards, that a man be found faithful. Required—not suggested. Because what is carried must be maintained.

Everything returns to the same conclusion. A mantle rests on structure, functions through capacity, produces stability, endures over time, and governs through order. None of these are received instantly. They are built. They are formed through pressure, time, and alignment.

Scripture does not show people chasing mantles. It shows people being formed until they could carry what was assigned to them.

THE MANTLES OF THE PROPHETS

Major, Minor, and the Governmental Mantle of Daniel.

A mantle is not defined by title. It is defined by function. This is why the prophets must be understood correctly. They were not cookie cutter and neither were their mantles. They were not carrying identical mantles. They were carrying different weights… with different assignments… requiring different structures.

All of them reveal the same truth: A mantle is proven by what it sustains.

THE MAJOR PROPHETS — WEIGHT THAT SHAPES NATIONS

Isaiah — The Revelatory Mantle

Isaiah did not carry a light word. He carried vision across generations. He spoke to power; he spoke to kings. God trusted him to speak the words of Judgment. He prophesied Redemption of man, and even the coming of Christ. His mantle required clarity of revelation, endurance over time, the ability to speak what was not yet visible. This is a mantle that sees far… and must remain steady while others do not understand what is being said.

Jeremiah — The Burdened Mantle

Jeremiah carried weight emotionally and spiritually. He spoke truth that people resisted. His mantle required endurance under rejection, emotional strength, consistency without validation. This is a mantle that does not rely on response. It speaks whether it is received or not.

Ezekiel — The Structural/Prophetic Symbolic Mantle

Ezekiel's mantle was not conventional. He *lived* the message. Symbolic acts. Visions. Embodied prophecy.

His mantle required obedience beyond understanding the ability to carry unusual instruction. His mantle required stability in the face of what others could not interpret. This is a mantle that **becomes the message**.

THE MINOR PROPHETS — PRECISION MANTLES

These are not "lesser" mantles; they are **focused mantles**.

Hosea — The Living Parable Mantle

Hosea did not just speak a message. He lived it. His life became the illustration of Israel's condition. This mantle required: personal sacrifice, obedience in uncomfortable assignments, and the ability to embody a message.

Amos — The Justice Mantle

Amos was not from the prophetic establishment. He was called from ordinary work. His mantle required boldness, clarity, and the refusal to soften truth. This is a mantle that confronts without needing position.

Jonah — The Reluctant Mantle

Jonah reveals that a mantle can be assigned even when the person resists it. A man's resistance does not remove responsibility. Jonah's life shows you can run, but you cannot escape what you are called to carry.

Daniel — THE GOVERNMENTAL MANTLE

Daniel is different. He was not just prophetic. He was governmental. He functioned inside systems of power. Kings. Empires. Decisions that affected nations. His mantle required consistency in hostile environments It required integrity under pressure, clarity of interpretation, and discipline over a lifetime.

Daniel did not have the luxury of stepping in and out. His mantle had to remain whether in public or in private. It didn't matter if he was in cris or in promotion. No matter the weight, it had to endure. This is a mantle that governs **within systems**, not outside of them.

None of these mantles were casual. They were no leisure suits, tracksuits or anything to lounge around in. They were not things to parade in either. None were received and instantly understood. None were carried without cost. Every one of them required structure, capacity, endurance, and alignment.

Different prophets. Different expressions… Same requirements. The difference in mantles is not the weight itself— it is the kind of life required to carry it.

If you study the prophets carefully… you will see people being formed until their lives could carry what had been assigned to them. This should give you pause to realize that all you've been through in your life is for this purpose. As Esther said, *For such a time as this*. Once all the becoming and the forming happened… there was no need to announce it, because what they carried spoke for itself.

Daniel is taken as a young man (likely a teenager). He undergoes 3 years of training. After those 3 years, he enters service in the king's court. Daniel did not arrive and immediately govern, receive authority instantly or step into position without formation. He was trained, tested, consistent, and sustained over decades.

Daniel did not rise in a moment. He was sustained over decades before he was entrusted with governance.

This supports capacity before addition, endurance as evidence.

Daniel's mantle was not proven early but sustained over time. He may have been around 60 years from captivity to high governmental authority. A governmental mantle is most often to govern in a foreign or formerly hostile land. ..

How shall we sing the LORD'S song in a strange land?
(Psalm 137:4)

That is not just emotion; it is dislocation. It is identity under pressure. It is assignment in an environment that does not agree with you.

Daniel answers that question with his life. Daniel never stopped functioning… even though he never left Babylon. He did not become Babylonian. He did not withdraw from responsibility.

He learned how to carry his mantle in a place that did not reflect his origin.

Psalm 137 is asking, How do we sing there? Daniel answers "You don't sing *to the land*—you remain aligned to God *in the land.*"

DANIEL'S PATTERN:

In Daniel 6:10: He prayed… with his windows open toward Jerusalem. He was physically in Babylon… but aligned somewhere else. That's the key.

Governmental mantles often function in strange places**.** This is the part people don't want: Joseph → Egypt. Daniel → Babylon. Esther → Persia. Influence came outside their original environment

Not because they lost identity… but because they maintained it under pressure.

A mantle is not proven in familiar places. It is revealed in environments that do not support it. Most people expect or think calling will lead to comfort. (*If only.*) They think assignment will lead to agreement. They think mantle will cause the alignment of environment. None of these things may automatically happen, even in a family. Even in a church.

Often, the mantle will lead to opposition, difference, and displacement.

The question is not, "Can I function here?" the question becomes, "Can I remain aligned here?" the declaration may have to become: I must remained aligned, and even here.

This is how you 'sing' in a strange land: You don't: adapt your identity, lower your structure, dissolve your alignment. You remain consistent, remain ordered, remain connected. Even when the environment is not.

Psalm 137 is the cry. Daniel is the answer.

You do not sing because the land is right. You remain because your alignment is.

NOT NAMED, BUT STILL CARRYING

Women In Scripture With Clear Mantles

Hannah — Intercession that produces destiny. Hannah was not loud. She was not public, but she was structurally powerful. Her mantle was intercession that births and sustains the prophet, Samuel. She didn't just pray once. She prayed, vowed, followed through, and not only continued covering; she had other children later.

Samuel did not just come from her womb. He came through her mantle.

Deborah — Governance and judgment. Deborah was a judge, leader, warrior, national authority. Her mantle was for governing order. Israel did not move without her word. She held structure, released instruction, and stabilized a nation.

Esther — Strategic intervention under pressure. She wasn't in constant visibility. But when she was needed she was precise with timed intervention. Her mantle was restraint, timing, courage under pressure. She carried weight in a moment that determined survival.

Abigail — Discernment that prevents destruction. She stepped **into a volatile situation and absorbed impact and redirected outcome. Her mantle** was discernment, de-escalation, and Wisdom under pressure. She stabilized what could have turned into bloodshed.

Mary (mother of Jesus) — Carrying what she did not create. Her mantle was the capacity to carry what came from God. She received, submitted, endured, and remained. She carried something she did not initiate, but had to sustain.

Anna — Sustained prophetic intercession. She spent decades in the temple fasting and in prayer. Her mantle long-term sustained devotion. She was enduring.

The Woman with the Issue of Blood — Faith that presses through. Her mantle expression was that she was relentless. She had focused faith. She endured, pressed, and acted. She didn't wait for structure—she moved toward it.

None of these women chased titles, announced mantles, or tried to become something publicly. They each carried something real.

A mantle is not determined by gender. It is revealed by what a life can carry. They did not receive *moments, but t*hey sustained weight.

WOMEN WITH HIDDEN / NON-OBVIOUS MANTLES

The Shunammite Woman — Discernment + Sustained Honor. She recognized Elisha without introduction. She built structure (a room), maintained it, honored consistently. When crisis came, she did not panic. She moved with clarity.

Her mantle was discernment that builds and sustains what God sends

The Widow of Zarephath — Obedience under lack. She had almost nothing, yet she obeyed under pressure. She gave from lack and remained consistent. Her mantle was sustaining life under impossible conditions.

The Wise Woman of Abel — Strategic preservation. A city was about to be destroyed. She assessed quickly, spoke wisely, and resolved the threat. She did this without position, and without title.

Her mantle was strategic intervention that preserves structure.

Huldah — Quiet prophetic authority. When the Book of the Law was found… they didn't go to Jeremiah, They went to her. She had no platform and no introduction. She did have recognized authority.

Her mantle was established truth without self-promotion.

Lydia — Structure that supports movement. She received truth, opened her home, created structure that supported the early church. Her mantle was creating environments where movement can grow.

Dorcas (Tabitha) — Tangible impact. Not preaching. Not leading publicly. But clothing people, meeting needs, consistent service. When she died the community felt the loss immediately. Her mantle was sustaining people through consistent provision.

The Midwives (Shiphrah & Puah) — Fear of God over systems. No platform. No visibility. But they resisted a corrupt system, preserved life, feared God over authority.

Their mantle was protecting life under pressure.

None of these women were visible leaders. None were publicly affirmed or widely announced. But, look at God; they were structurally essential.

Some mantles are not seen in position. They are revealed in what would collapse if they were removed.

They did not: carry influence, but they held things together.

JOHN THE BAPTIST — A MANTLE WITHOUT DEFENSE

John did not build a platform. He did not establish an institution. He did not create a system that pointed to himself. He was sent with one assignment: prepare the way.

That was the mantle. Not broad. Not scattered. Precise.

> I am the voice of one crying in the wilderness, Make straight the way of the Lord. (John 1:23)

Notice, he did not say who he thought he was. He stated what he was sent to do.

In John 1:20–21, they asked him, "Are you the Christ? Are you Elijah? Are you that prophet?" He answered plainly, "I am not." There was no insistence, no inflation, and no defense, because his mantle did not require it.

This reveals something essential. A real mantle is clear in function. It is stable in identity. It does not need to be expanded artificially. John did not try to become more. He remained exactly what he was assigned to be.

John's mantle also had a boundary. It ended where Christ was revealed. In John 3:30, he said, "He must increase, but I must decrease." That is not loss. That is alignment.

A real mantle knows where it begins, and it knows where it ends.

There was no competition. John did not compete with what came after him. He did not try to maintain relevance. He did not attempt to hold position, because his mantle was never about permanence. It was about completion of assignment.

What he governed was preparation, alignment, and readiness. He did not govern people long-term. He governed transition.

Not every mantle is meant to last indefinitely. Some are meant to prepare what comes next.

John did not declare himself repeatedly. He did not defend his position. He did not argue for recognition, because what he carried was already evident in what he did.

A mantle that must be defended is not yet established. John carried one that only needed to be fulfilled. He had authority. He had recognition. He had followers. And still, he did not build around himself. That is rare.

John did not stand alone. He stood at a transition—a point where one assignment ended and another began. John's mantle was not to remain. It was to prepare.

In John 1:29, he said, "Behold the Lamb of God." He did not draw attention to himself. He directed it, because his mantle was not the destination. It was the introduction.

Where John prepared, Christ established. Christ did not operate within a mantle that required confirmation from others. He operated from Authority itself. He said,

> All power is given unto me in heaven and in earth.
> (Matthew 28:18)

This is the shift—from preparation to establishment. This is where many become confused. They attempt to operate as if nothing changed, as if authority is still undefined, as if it still needs to be discovered. But after Christ, authority was not left open. It was established.

After the Cross, mantles did not disappear, but their function became clear. They no longer establish authority. They operate under it.

A mantle now does not create authority. It does not compete for position. It functions within what has already been established. This is why alignment matters. A mantle that is not aligned with what has been established in Christ cannot be sustained, because it is not supported by the foundation that now governs.

After the Cross, assignments continue. Functions continue. Responsibilities continue. But they are no longer independent, undefined, or self-established. They are aligned, structured, and accountable.

The difference in operation is clear. Before, there was preparation for what was coming. Now, there is function within what has been established. Many seek identity, authority, and validation as if it has not already been defined. But the question is no longer, "Is there authority?" The question is, "Are you aligned with it?"

John prepared what was coming. Christ established what is. After the Cross, mantles function within that reality.

A mantle no longer points to what is coming. It must align with what has already been established.

This removes confusion about the origin of authority and clarifies that modern mantles are functional, not foundational.

THEY CARRIED THEIR MANTLES

Notable Modern Day Examples

Billy Graham served for decades of consistent function. His message stayed focused. He avoided major public collapse. Mantle expression: sustained evangelistic clarity over time. He didn't expand into everything. He remained in what he was assigned; evangelism.

Mother Teresa demonstrated long-term consistency in one lane. She was not platform-driven. She endured internal struggle but continued on. Her mantle expression was endurance in service without withdrawal.

Elisabeth Elliot showed that the weight of loss did not break function. She continued teaching with clarity. She stayed aligned after trauma. Her mantle expression was stability after disruption

A.W. Tozer lived a disciplined life. He had a deep internal formation. His message consistent across years. His mantle expression was depth over display.

Corrie ten Boom endured extreme pressure. She continued in forgiveness message. She did not collapse under history. Her mantle expression was continuing to carry truth after suffering

Then there are times when something starts… but doesn't hold.

Ravi Zacharias had a strong global teaching influence. He displayed intellectual clarity, and had a wide platform. After his death, there were credible investigations that revealed long-term misconduct. He functioned well publicly, but the structure was not sustained privately.

Jim Bakker had a rapid rise and a massive platform with influence and visibility. Then there was financial scandal, moral failure and the ultimate collapse of his ministry. Expansion exceeded structure.

Ted Haggard had a very large congregation with national influence. Then there was the exposure of hidden behavior and his immediate removal.

What is not aligned will eventually be revealed under weight.

Mark Driscoll showed a strong leadership presence with rapid church growth. Then internal dysfunction showed itself. Leadership pressure issues were exposed and the organization collapsed. Growth without sustainable structure will fragment over time.

Weight reveals what was not built. Something real may have started. Something effective may have functioned, but it did not sustain. What begins in strength must be sustained in structure. A mantle does not fail. A life can become misaligned with it.

I've shared these examples to show what happens when the weight of a mantle is not upheld. Starting is not the measure; sustaining is.

No modern example is perfect, some were worse than others and some totally collapsed. But there are many good people who are widely regarded as having carried something without abandoning it.

All of these showed consistency over time. They were in full alignment with their assignments. None of them showed visible collapse under *weight*. A mantle is not proven by how it begins, it is revealed by how it finishes.

Finish well.

THE END

I seal these words decrees, declarations and prayers across every dimension and timeline, past, present, and future, to infinity, in the Name of Jesus.

I seal them with the Blood of Jesus and the Holy Spirit of Promise.

Any retaliation against this author, the reader or anyone who prays these prayers, makes these decrees and declarations at any time, let that retaliation backfire on the head of the perpetrator to infinity, and without Mercy, in the Name of Jesus.

Dear Reader

Thank you for acquiring this book and supporting this ministry. I pray this book has accomplished what it set out to do--, teach you about Godly mantles.

Shalom,

Dr. Marlene Miles

New Releases:

Christ of God (*The*) 3-book series

Christ of God, (*The*) Box Set, includes all 3 books

Prayerbooks by this author

There are some books that are only prayers. You just open up the book and pray.

FAKE FRIENDS: *Prayers Against Betrayers*

HOLIDAY WARFARE Prayer Manual (humorous) Surviving Family Gatherings All Year Long (without catching a case)

SOUL TIE Prayer Manual (The) Part of a 3-part series including a workbook.

MAD at DADDY Prayer Manual – part of a 3-part series including a workbook.

Healing the Sibling & Relative Wound Prayer Manual

Healing the Father-Son Wound Prayer Manual

Prayers Against Barrenness: *For Success in Business and Life*

Breaking Curses of the Mother Prayer Manual

Prayers Against Barrenness: *For Success in Business and Life*

Fruit of the Womb: *Prayers Against Barrenness*

Beauty Curses, *Warfare Prayers Against*
https://a.co/d/5Xlc2OM

Courts of Marriage: Prayers for Marriage in the Courts of Heaven *(prayerbook)* https://a.co/d/cNAdgAq

Courtroom Warfare @ Midnight *(prayerbook)*
https://a.co/d/5fc7Qdp

Demonic Cobwebs *(prayerbook)* https://a.co/d/fp9Oa2H

Every Evil Bird https://a.co/d/hF1kh1O

Gates of Thanksgiving

Spirits of Death, Hell & the Grave, Pass Over Me and My House

Throne of Grace: Courtroom Prayer

Warfare Prayer Against Poverty
https://a.co/d/bZ61lYu

Other books by this author

Abundance of Jesus (The) https://a.co/d/5gHJVed

AK: The Adventures of the Agape Kid

Already Married in the Spirit: *Why You May Not Be Married in the Natural*

AMONG SOME THIEVES https://a.co/d/dkYT4ZV

Ancestral Powers

Anti-Karen: *How To Mind Your Own Business Without Minding Other People's*

Anti-Marriage, *The Spirit of*

Backstabbers https://a.co/d/gi8iBxf

Barrenness, *Prayers Against* https://a.co/d/feUltIs

Battlefield of Marriage, *The*

Beware of the Dog: Prayers Against Dogs in the Dream.

Bless Your Food: *Let the Dining Table be Undefiled* *https://a.co/d/6oPMRDv*

Blindsided: *Has the Old Man Bewitched You?* https://a.co/d/5O2fLLR

Break Free from Collective Captivity

Broken Spirits & Dry Bones

By Means of a Whorish Father

Caged Life: Get Out Alive! https://a.co/d/bwPbksX

Casting Down Imaginations

Christ of God (*The*) 3-book series

Christ of God, (*The*) Box Set, includes all 3 books

Churchzilla, The Wanna-Be, Supposed-to-be Bride of Christ https://a.co/d/eAf5j3x

Collateral Damage: *When What Happened Spiritually Was Your Fault*

Deep Poverty: Get Out of Poverty and Its Shame

Demonic Cobwebs (prayerbook)

Demonic Time Bombs

Demons Hate Questions

Devil Loves Trauma, *The*

Devil Weapons: Unforgiveness, Bitterness,...

The Devourers: Thieves of Darkness 2

Do Not Swear by the Moon

Don't Refuse Me, Lord (4 book series)

https://a.co/d/idP34LG

Dream Defilement

The Emptiers: *Thieves of Darkness, 1*
https://a.co/d/5I4n5mc

Entanglements:

Evil Touch

Failed Assignment

Fantasy Spirit Spouse https://a.co/d/hW7oYbX

FAT Demons (The): *Breaking Demonic Curses* https://a.co/d/4kP8wV1

The Fold (5-book series)

- The Fold (Book 1)
- Name Your Seed (Book 2)
- The Poor Attitudes of Money (3)
- Do Not Orphan Your Seed (4)
- For the Sake of the Gospel (5)
- My Sowing Journal

Gang Ups: Touch Not God's Anointed

Gathered: No Longer Scattered https://a.co/d/1i5DPIX

Getting Rid of Evil Spiritual Food https://a.co/d/i2L3WYQ

got HEALING? Verses for Life

got LOVE? Verses for Life https://a.co/d/8seXHPd

got HOPE? Verses for Life

got money? https://a.co/d/g2av41N

Has My Soul Been Sold? https://a.co/d/dyB8hhA

Here Come the Horns: *Skilled to Destroy* https://a.co/d/cZiNnkP

Hidden Sins: Hidden Iniquity

https://a.co/d/4Mth0wa

How to Dental Assist

How to Dental Assist2: Be Productive, Not Wasteful

How To Stay Prayed Up

How to STOP Being a Blind Witch or Warlock

I Take It Back

In Multiplying I Will Multiply Thee

Into Freedom:

Irresistible: Jesus' Triumphal Entry https://a.co/d/d09IfEC

KNOW YOUR BATTLE: Stop Swinging Blindly — and Win Against Opponents, Adversaries & Enemies (Workbook) https://a.co/d/eOwFKlV

Legacy

Let Me Have A Dollar's Worth
https://a.co/d/h8F8XgE

Level the Playing Field

Living for the NOW of God https://a.co/d/6bK5duE

Lose My Location https://a.co/d/crD6mV9

Love Breaks Your Heart

Mad At Daddy: Healing Father-Wounds that Affect Motherhood (book, workbook & prayer manual)

Made Perfect In Love

Mammon https://a.co/d/29yhMG7

Man Safari, *The*

Marriage Ed.: *Rules of Engagement & Marriage*

Made Perfect in Love

Money Hunters: Beware of Those

Money on the Altar https://a.co/d/4EqJ2Nr

Mulberry Tree, *The* https://a.co/d/9nR9rRb

Motherboard (The)- *Soul Prosperity Series*

Name Your Seed

Occupy: *Until I Return* https://a.co/d/bZ7ztUy

One Defining Day*: A Day When Dreams Come True*

Opponent, Adversary, or Enemy?: Fight The Right Battle with the Right Weapons

https://a.co/d/byQqEE2 & companion workbook: Know Your Battle

Plantation Souls

Players Gonna Play

Portals: Shut the Front Door: Prayers to Close Evil Portals.

Power Money: Nine Times the Tithe

https://a.co/d/gRt41gy

The Power to Get Wealth https://a.co/d/e4ub4Ov

Powers Above

The Robe, Part 1, The Lessons of Joseph

The Robe, Part II, The Lessons of Joseph

Seasons of Grief

Seasons of Siege: God Is Coming

Seasons of Waiting

Seasons of War

Second Marriage, Third--, *Any Marriage*

https://a.co/d/6m6GN4N

Seducing Spirits: Idolatry & Whoredoms

https://a.co/d/4Jq4WEs

Shut the Front Door: *Prayers to Close Portals* https://a.co/d/cH4TWJj

Siege: *God Is Coming*

Sift You Like Wheat

Six Men Short: What Has Happened to all the Men?

SLAVE

Sleep Afflictions & Really Bad Dreams https://a.co/d/f8sDmgv

Soul Prosperity soul prosperity series 3

https://a.co/d/5p8YvCN

Soul Ties: How Soul Ties Form, and How To Break Them (book, workbook & prayer manual)

Souls In Captivity

The Spirit of Anti-Marriage

The Spirit of Poverty https://a.co/d/abV2o2e

Spiritual Thieves https://a.co/d/eqPPz33

StarStruck- Triangular Power series.

SUNBLOCK- Triangular Power series.

The Swallowers: *Thieves of Darkness*, 3

Take It Back

This Is NOT That: How to Keep Demons from Coming at You

Time Is of the Essence

Too Many Wives: *Why You Have Lady Problems*

Tormenting Spirits https://a.co/d/dAogEJf

Toxic Souls

Triangular Power *(series),* Powers Above, SUNBLOCK, Do Not Swear by the Moon, TARSTRUCK

TRIBE: *What Covenants Are Governing You…?*

Unbreak My Heart: *Don't Let Me Die*

Uncontested Doom

Ungovered Hunger: How Unchecked Appetite Dismantles Authority

Unguarded Hours, *The*

Unseen Life, *The* (forthcoming)

Upgrade: How to Get Out of Survival Mode Toxic Souls (Book 2 of series) , Legacy (Book 3 of series)

The Wasters: *Thieves of Darkness,* Bk 2 https://a.co/d/bUvI9Jo

What Have You to Declare? What Do You Have With You from Where You've Been?

When I Was A Child, *I Prayed As a Child*

When the Devourer is Rebuked https://a.co/d/1HVv8oq

When The Table Is Set Against You

WTH? Get Me Out of This Hell https://a.co/d/a7WBGJh

The Wilderness Romance ***(series)*** This series is about conducting a Godly relationship and marriage with someone who is a Wilderness person. ***The Social Wilderness***

- ***The Sexual Wilderness***
- ***The Spiritual Wilderness***

Other Series

The Fold (a series on Godly finances)

https://a.co/d/4hz3unj

Soul Prosperity Series https://a.co/d/bz2M42q

Spirit Spouse books

https://a.co/d/9VehDSo

https://a.co/d/97sKOwm

Battlefield of Marriage, The https://a.co/d/eUDzizO

Players Gonna Play

https://a.co/d/2hzGw3N

Sent Spirit Spouse (can someone send you a spirit spouse? This book is not yet released.)

Thieves of Darkness series

The Emptiers https://a.co/d/heio0dO

The Wasters https://a.co/d/5TG1iNQ

The Swallowers https://a.co/d/1jWhM6G

The Devourers: Why We Can't Have Nice Things https://a.co/d/87Tejbf

Dr. Marlene Miles is a teacher, author, and spiritual thinker known for her grounded, discerning approach to prayer and spiritual formation. Her work emphasizes clarity, restraint, and maturity in faith—helping believers move beyond emotionalism and performance into a steady, practiced walk with God.

With a deep respect for Scripture and a practical understanding of daily life, Dr. Miles writes for those who want their prayer life to be formed, not dramatized. Her teaching encourages spiritual maintenance, discernment, and responsibility—so faith remains strong not only in crisis, but in everyday living.

www.ingramcontent.com/pod-product-compliance
Lightning Source LLC
LaVergne TN
LVHW010702110826
845149LV00014B/3200

* 9 7 8 1 9 7 1 9 3 3 5 4 2 *